GEORGIA O'KEEFFE AND NEW MEXICO

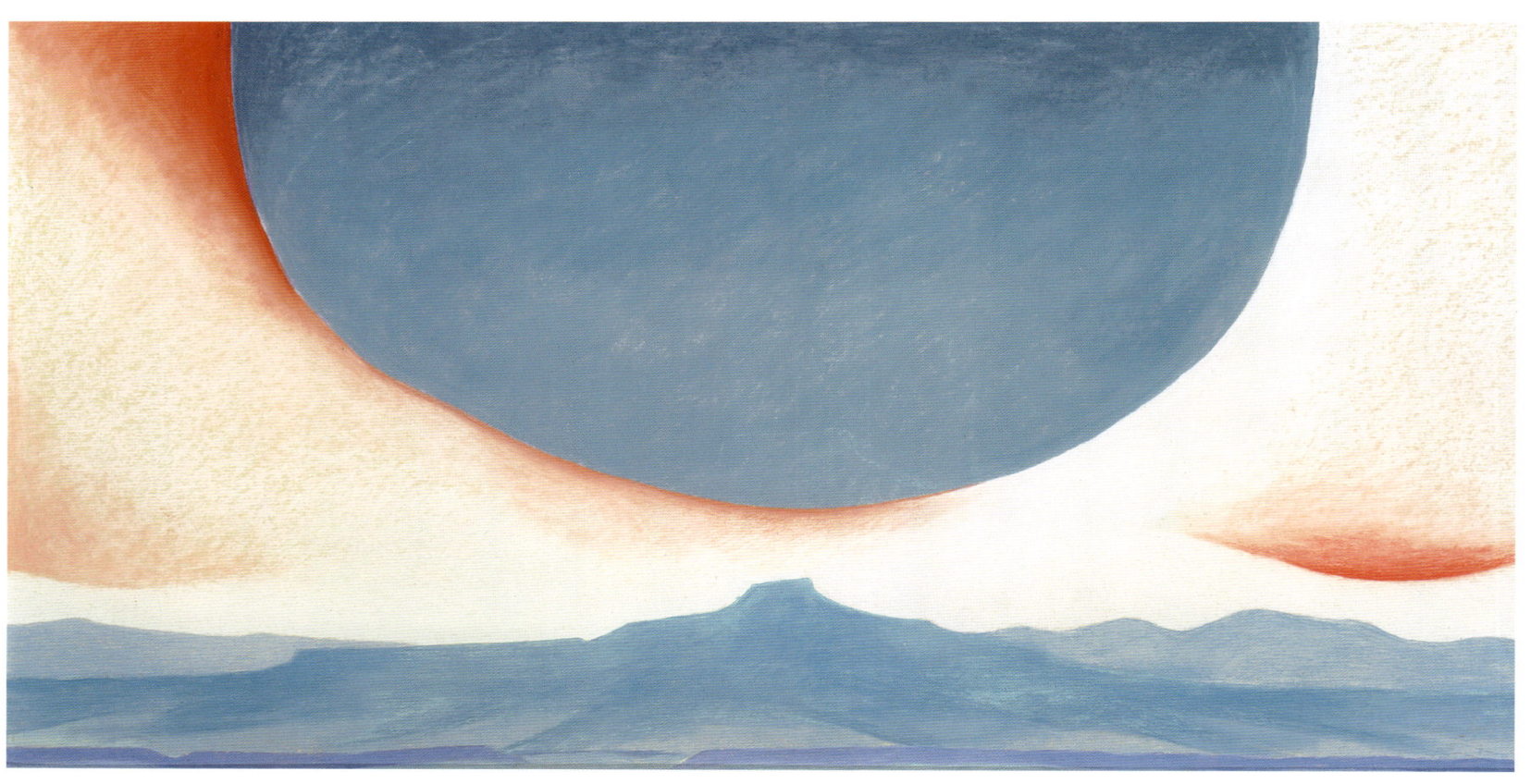

GEORGIA O'KEEFFE AND NEW MEXICO

■ A SENSE OF PLACE

BARBARA BUHLER LYNES

LESLEY POLING-KEMPES

AND FREDERICK W. TURNER

PRINCETON UNIVERSITY PRESS

Princeton and Oxford

GEORGIA O'KEEFFE MUSEUM

Santa Fe, New Mexico

Note about the captions: The captions for Georgia O'Keeffe's images contain catalogue raisonné numbers; these refer to entries in Lynes, *Georgia O'Keeffe: Catalogue Raisonné*, 1999.

Front cover: *Hill, New Mexico*, 1935 (CR 872; plate 3)

Back cover: *Black Place III*, 1944 (CR 1082; plate 17)

Frontispiece: *Pedernal*, 1945 (CR 1117; checklist no. 48)

Published by Princeton University Press in association with the Georgia O'Keeffe Museum on the occasion of the exhibition *Georgia O'Keeffe and New Mexico: A Sense of Place*.

The exhibition and its accompanying catalogue have been made possible by generous support from The Burnett Foundation and the National Council of the Georgia O'Keeffe Museum.

Princeton University Press, 41 William Street, Princeton, New Jersey 08540
In the United Kingdom: Princeton University Press, 3 Market Place, Woodstock, Oxfordshire OX20 1SY
pup.princeton.edu

Georgia O'Keeffe Museum
217 Johnson Street, Santa Fe, New Mexico 87501

EXHIBITION TOUR
Georgia O'Keeffe Museum, Santa Fe, New Mexico, June 11–September 12, 2004
Columbus Museum of Art, Ohio, October 1, 2004–January 16, 2005
Delaware Art Museum, Wilmington, February 17–May 15, 2005

Printed and bound in Italy

15

Library of Congress Cataloging-in-Publication Data

Lynes, Barbara Buhler
   Georgia O'Keeffe and New Mexico : a sense of place / Barbara Buhler Lynes, Lesley Poling-Kempes, and Frederick W. Turner.
      p. cm.
   Catalog of an exhibition held at the Georgia O'Keeffe Museum, June 11–Sept. 12, 2004, the Columbus Museum of Art, Oct. 1, 2004–Jan. 16, 2005, and the Delaware Art Museum, Feb. 17–May 15, 2005.
   Includes bibliographical references and index.
   ISBN 0-691-11659-8 (cloth : alk. paper)
      1. O'Keeffe, Georgia, 1887–1986—Exhibitions. 2. Landscape in art—Exhibitions. 3. New Mexico—In art—Exhibitions. I. Poling-Kempes, Lesley. II. Turner, Frederick W., 1937– III. Georgia O'Keeffe Museum. IV. Columbus Museum of Art. V. Delaware Art Museum. VI. Title.

ND237.O5A4 2004
759.13—dc22   2003062202

ISBN-13: 978-0-691-11659-4 (cloth)
ISBN-10: 0-691-11659-8 (cloth)

Contents

DIRECTOR'S FOREWORD   7

GEORGIA O'KEEFFE AND NEW MEXICO: A SENSE OF PLACE   11
BARBARA BUHLER LYNES

A SENSE OF PLACE I:
TAOS, ALCALDE, TIERRA AZUL, GHOST RANCH, BLACK PLACE   59

A CALL TO PLACE   77
LESLEY POLING-KEMPES

A SENSE OF PLACE II:
CHAMA RIVER, WHITE PLACE, ABIQUIU, GHOST RANCH   89

ON HER CONQUEST OF SPACE   109
FREDERICK W. TURNER

CHRONOLOGY   125
CHECKLIST   128
SUGGESTIONS FOR FURTHER READING   134
ACKNOWLEDGMENTS   136
INDEX   138
PHOTOGRAPHY CREDITS   143

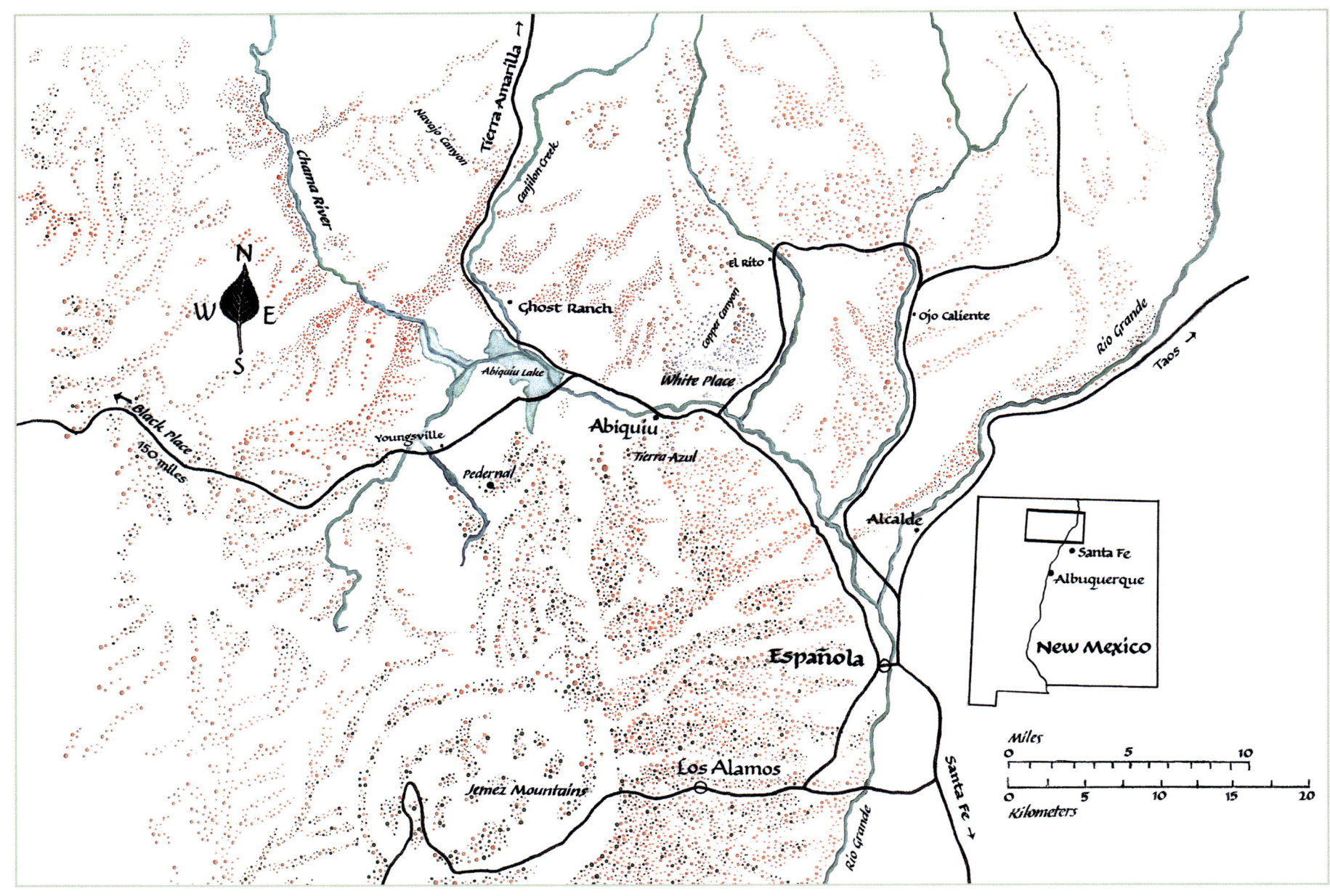

Chama River

Navajo Canyon

Tierra Amarilla ↑

Canjilon Creek

El Rito

Ghost Ranch

Copper Canyon

Ojo Caliente

Rio Grande

N
W E
S

Abiquiu Lake

White Place

Taos →

Black Place
150 miles

Youngsville

Abiquiu

Tierra Azul

Pedernal

Alcalde

Española

• Santa Fe
• Albuquerque

New Mexico

Los Alamos

Jemez Mountains

Rio Grande

Santa Fe →

Miles
0   5   10

0   5   10   15   20
Kilometers

Georgia O'Keeffe and New Mexico: A Sense of Place is the first exhibition organized around the artist's works interpreting the New Mexico landscape to which she was so passionately attached. Like other notable creative individuals who have concentrated on one particularly compelling phenomenon, O'Keeffe produced a body of work that is subtle, remarkable, and unique. She is internationally recognized for her broad range of work spanning many decades, but in fact it is her depictions of the land in this strikingly beautiful state that have rooted her permanently in the minds of her public.

The Museum is proud to have organized this important exhibition, which further advances its mission to place the artist in the broader context of American modernism. We do this by originating exhibitions that focus exclusively on O'Keeffe as well as by organizing projects that include work by many of her contemporaries and artists active today.

I am grateful to Barbara Buhler Lynes, Curator, Georgia O'Keeffe Museum, and The Emily Fisher Landau Director of the Museum's Research Center, for her insightful scholarship on this project and her continued passion for and discoveries in the exceptional life and art of Georgia O'Keeffe. Lynes's fine essay, along with those by Lesley Poling-Kempes and Frederick W. Turner, provide perceptive and informative views about the sites that O'Keeffe so favored and that still exist intact today.

Even though the Museum does own the largest single collection of O'Keeffe works, we nonetheless must rely on the generosity of our lenders to complete our projects. And because the exhibition will be on view in three venues I am especially grateful to all who have committed their important loans to the entire run of the exhibition.

I would like to thank the staff and directors at each institution that will host the exhibition after it closes at this Museum. At the Columbus Museum of Art in Ohio, former Director Irving Lippman expressed enthusiasm early on in the project, and at the Delaware Art Museum, Director Stephen Bruni and his staff were also eager to have their audience benefit from a showing in their state.

Lastly, the Museum could not realize exhibitions of this scope without the support of many of its patrons. In particular I would like to thank the members of the Board of Directors of The Burnett Foundation and the National Council of the Georgia O'Keeffe Museum for their generosity and affirmation of this particularly important and exciting project.

George G. King
Director, Georgia O'Keeffe Museum

GEORGIA O'KEEFFE AND NEW MEXICO

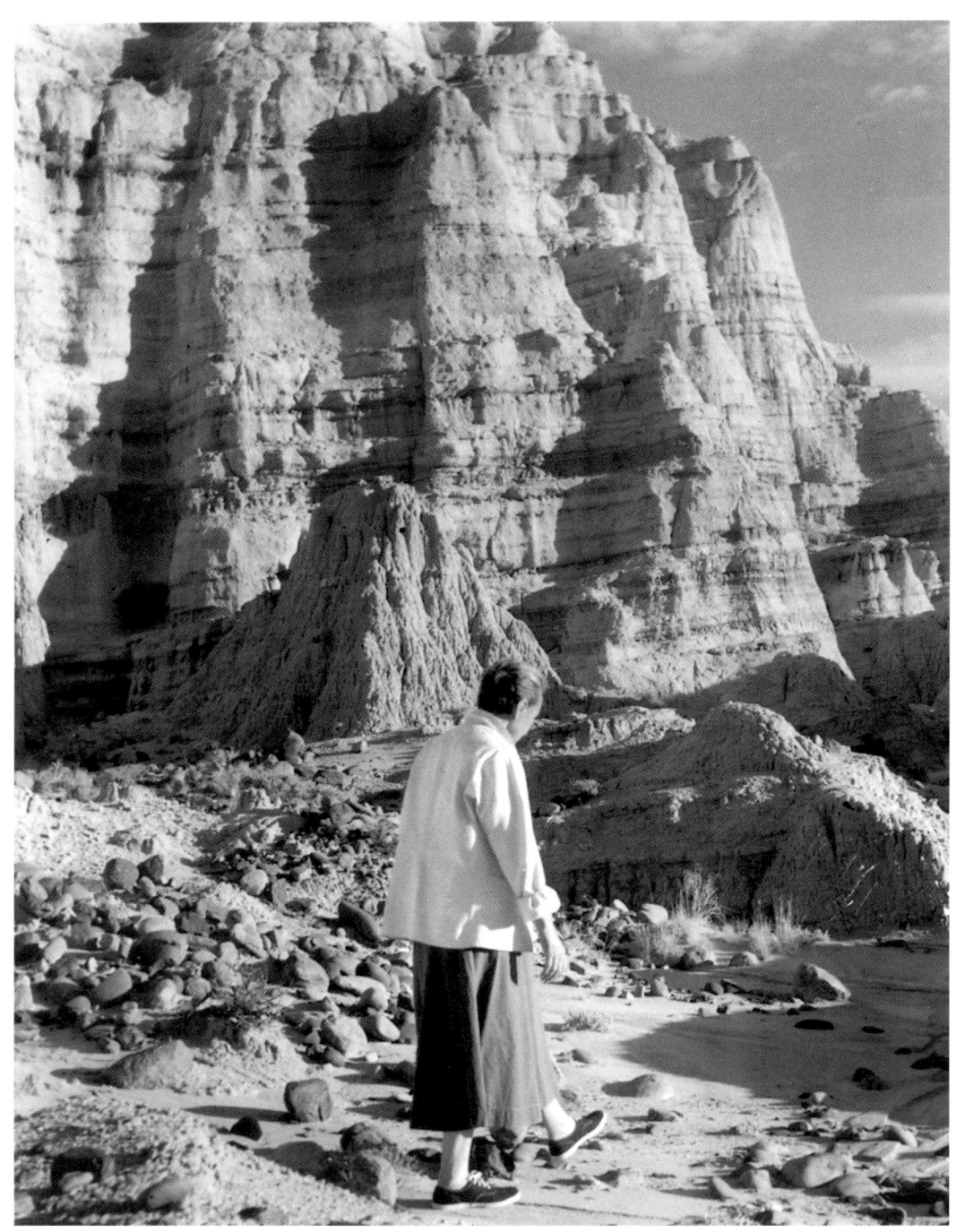

GEORGIA O'KEEFFE AND NEW MEXICO: A SENSE OF PLACE

BARBARA BUHLER LYNES

AT THE TIME of her first major exhibition in 1916, Georgia O'Keeffe was working almost exclusively as an abstractionist, and over the next two years, when she was living either in Texas or Virginia, she produced approximately seventy abstractions derived from landscape subject matter. But after she moved to New York in 1918 and before 1929, when she began spending part of each year in New Mexico, she produced fewer than thirty abstractions that definitely can be said to have sources in the landscape. During this same eleven-year period, O'Keeffe also made about twenty works that can be called landscapes—mainly of subject matter at Lake George, where she spent most summers and falls—but although their forms are quite generalized, these works must be considered representational.

These landscapes reflect a general shift toward the objective that occurred in the body of O'Keeffe's work in the early 1920s, primarily in response to critical interpretations of her abstractions that linked them with her sexual nature.[1] She never abandoned abstraction, and her representational paintings are replete with abstract components, but by the mid-twenties, aided by the apparent heightened "realism" of her large-scale flower paintings, O'Keeffe had redefined herself primarily as a painter of recognizable forms, and she remains so defined today in the public eye.[2]

OPPOSITE, FIG. I
Todd Webb, *O'Keeffe Walking in The White Place, Abiquiu, NM,* 1955

Her paintings of the New Mexico landscape from the 1930s and 1940s are among her best known. The sobriquet "O'Keeffe country" is often used to describe the large section of northwestern New Mexico from which the artist drew inspiration, but it is probably best applied to the area around Ghost Ranch, where she lived and worked part of every year for almost half a century. The term implies how thoroughly O'Keeffe's exploration of this landscape made it her own; and indeed she felt a proprietary relationship to elements within it, as can be seen in the titles of certain paintings and in statements she made over the years.

When I first visited Ghost Ranch, which lies at the southeastern end of the Chama River Valley, some sixty miles northwest of Santa Fe, I was overwhelmed by the visual complexity and violent geological history of the area—a vast panorama of contrasting forms and colors shaped over millions of years by water and wind erosion. More particularly, I immediately recognized some of the sites that had inspired paintings O'Keeffe made there more than seventy years ago, and I became aware of the varying degrees to which the forms in these paintings refer with seeming realism to the sites' contours, proportions, and colors.

Moreover, when I explored these sites, walking in and around them, I found I could pinpoint where O'Keeffe had positioned herself to achieve the configurations in several of her paintings. These observations made me want to explore further the degree to which she re-created the forms in her New Mexico landscapes exactly as she saw them; in other words, the degree to which the forms in her drawings and paintings of these subjects were specific to the sites that informed them. Certainly, at first glance these works appear to be site-specific—seemingly precise references to identifiable landscape forms—and thus far removed in concept from the landscape-derived abstractions of her early career and even the Lake George landscapes, with their pervasive abstract elements. But I wondered if these works were truly site-specific, and if so, how this realization might affect my perception of the larger body of O'Keeffe's work, which I perceived as having strong abstract underpinnings.

O'Keeffe frequently wrote letters from New Mexico that not only describe exactly where she was, but also often mention what she was painting. With this information and reproductions of her works in hand, I traveled to various places she had worked in New Mexico. I discovered more than sixty sites that had inspired particular paintings, made study photographs of them, and later commissioned professional photographs of twenty sites that were made from points of view that represent, as faithfully as possible, those presented in O'Keeffe's paintings.[3] After comparing the photographs with the paintings, I decided to organize an exhibition that would demonstrate the relationships that exist between subject and object and thereby both chart the frequency with which site specificity occurs in O'Keeffe's New Mexico landscapes and define its significance to her work.

In almost all of her landscape paintings of the 1930s and 1940s, O'Keeffe's reliance on contour as a descriptive device permits her to present specific, recognizable landscape configurations as sharply focused, fixed entities. This infuses her work with a sense of precision that, regardless of her inventions, gives it a quality of verisimilitude. It is not surprising then that others have noted this and, in analyzing the phenomenon, have suggested that this seemingly heightened "realism" represents a development distinctive to her landscape paintings of these decades.[4]

Yet these works are the opposite of verisimilitude. Paintings that may appear at first to adhere faithfully to their subjects are, in fact, highly subjective explorations that are as dependent on the manipulation of color and shape as they are on the forms that inspired them. And in spite of the fact that almost all of these paintings depict certain components of specific sites with amazing accuracy, they as consistently use the sites as a framework for exploring various formal devices with which O'Keeffe had experimented for years. In so doing, she selectively manipulated the forms she saw in New Mexico landscapes to achieve some of the most inventive and imaginative works of her career. In what follows, I compare a number of paintings to the site photographs in order to demonstrate that, in spite of their apparent specificity, O'Keeffe's New Mexico landscapes reveal her lifelong commitment to abstraction.

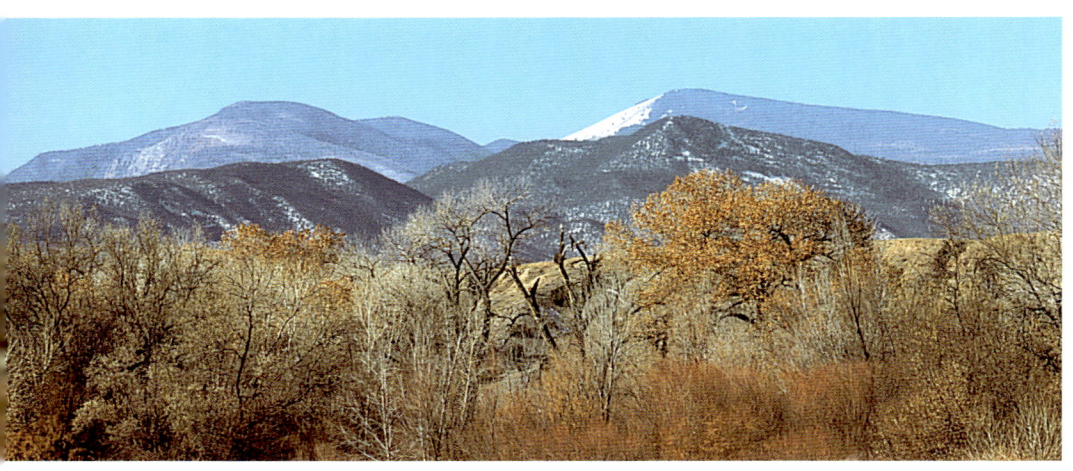

Photograph of site of *Black Mesa Landscape, New Mexico / Out Back of Marie's II* (plate 1)

Black Mesa Landscape, New Mexico / Out Back of Marie's II,
1930
Oil on canvas
24 1/4 x 36 1/4 in. (65.1 x 92.1 cm)
Georgia O'Keeffe Museum,
Santa Fe, N. Mex. Gift of The
Burnett Foundation
CR 730

O'KEEFFE MADE THIS PAINTING (plate 1) during her second summer in New Mexico, when she was staying in Alcalde as a guest at the H. and M. Ranch, owned by her friend Marie Tudor Garland. It represents a very small section of the landscape, which O'Keeffe isolated from the vast panorama of mountains, hills, and cliffs she saw to the west from the ranch. Where the sky meets the land in both the painting and the photograph of this site (fig. 2), there is almost an exact correspondence between the contours of the two major peaks of the Jemez range and the top of a more distant mountain that rises between them. These forms change shape and the small peak between the two large mountain forms disappears if one's point of view shifts slightly to the north or south.

The contours of the mountains just below the tallest peaks appear in the photograph exactly as O'Keeffe depicted them, but the blue and brown undulating hills just below the mountains as well as the red hills below those can no longer be seen. The view has been partially obscured by the trees that have grown significantly since 1930, when she depicted them as a thin horizontal band in her composition. A photograph taken farther west, beyond both the trees and the red hills, indicates that the painting accurately records the contours of the landscape's more distant hills. The slightly higher vantage point in the painting can be explained by the fact that O'Keeffe recorded the view as she saw it from the roof of the Garland house.

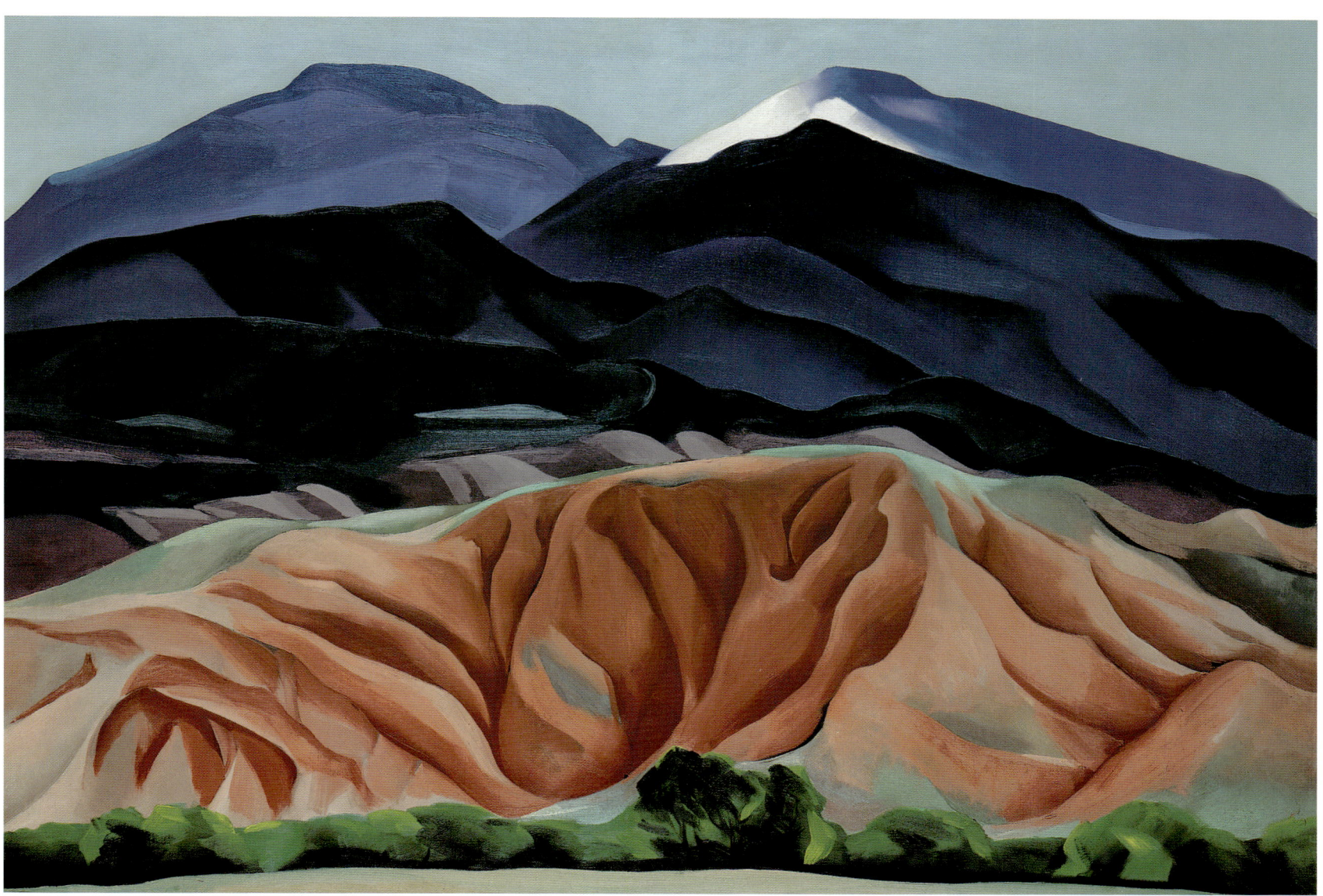

It is clear that O'Keeffe almost literally transcribed the contours of the forms she saw, but it is equally clear that she freely changed their sizes. The peak on the left, for example, becomes a much taller and larger element in the painting than it is in the actual landscape, and O'Keeffe also reduced the size of the dark-blue mountain directly below the snow-covered peak. Similar manipulations occur as we move downward in the composition. For example, she enlarged the red hills so that they occupy almost half of the composition, while in the actual landscape they are far less dominant. Finally, although the photograph demonstrates that all of these forms are situated within a deeply receding space, O'Keeffe manipulated their scale so that the forms in the distance occupy approximately the same amount of compositional space as the red hills. This, as well as the very ambiguous transition between the red hills and the blue mountains, helps bring them into a nearly contiguous relationship, thus effectually eliminating the idea of spatial recession.

O'Keeffe made frequent excursions by car from the H. and M. Ranch to nearby areas. In Tierra Azul, about fourteen miles north of Alcalde toward Abiquiu, on the west side of the road she found these three buff-colored sand hills that rise in isolation from the relatively flat ground around them. At first glance these hills seem to be replicated rather exactly in *New Mexican Landscape* (plate 2), but a closer inspection of the photograph of them (fig. 3) in relationship to the painting reveals the many adjustments that O'Keeffe made to their sizes, shapes, and internal contours.

In the painting, the top of the left hill rises more steeply than it does in the actual landscape, and its top is more pointed and prominent. O'Keeffe also shortened the distance between this form and the hill to its right by eliminating the small bump that can be seen between the two forms in the landscape. Moreover, she edited the contour of the slope that separates the smaller hills in the painting, giving it an angularity that does not appear in the photograph. It might seem that if one moved slightly to the left to photograph these hills, the resulting view would correspond exactly to the one in O'Keeffe's painting. But what O'Keeffe ostensibly recorded does not exist in nature. In viewing the hills from various points to the left, the shape and position of the largest hill change, no longer conforming to the nearly frontal view in the painting.

This work also reveals O'Keeffe's keen interest in the reduction and simplification of forms. She eliminated nearly all of the trees on the hills (whose current abundance suggests that many more than she recorded existed in 1930), and she made no reference to the roughness or uneven surface textures they give to the hills. Rather, these slopes exist in the painting as smooth forms—flattened planes of muted color. Such manipulations have the effect of denying volume and compressing space, making what is volumetric seem flat and what is distant seem close.

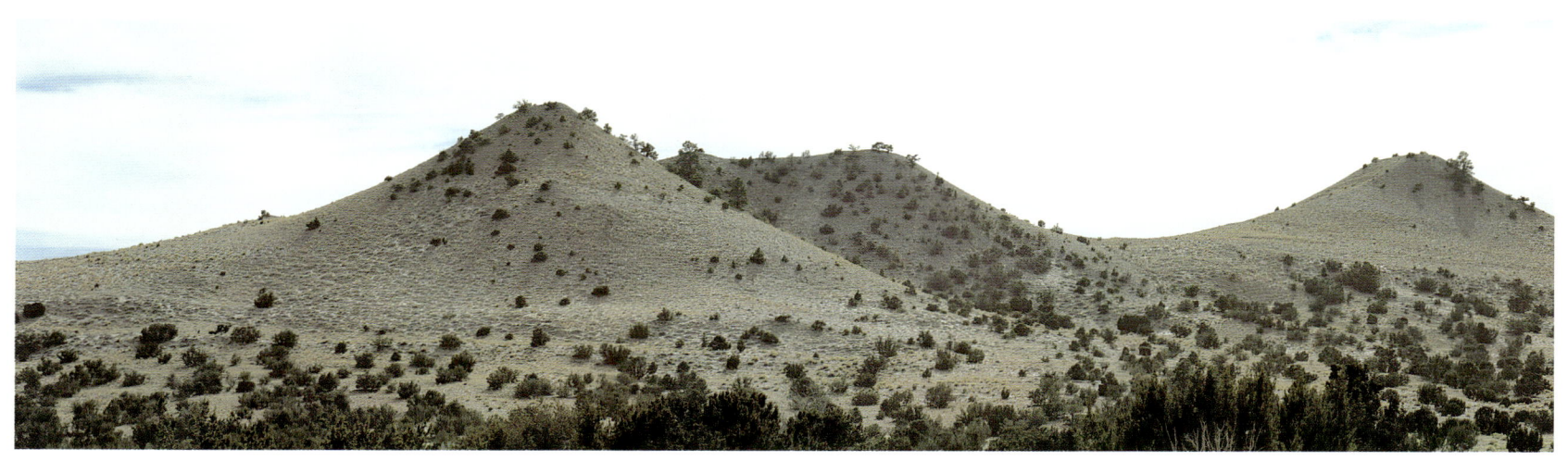

ABOVE, FIG. 3
Photograph of site of *New Mexican Landscape* (plate 2)

OPPOSITE, PLATE 2
New Mexican Landscape, 1930
Oil on canvas
16 x 30 in. (40.6 x 76.2 cm)
Museum of Fine Arts,
Springfield, Mass. James Philip
Gray Collection
CR 732

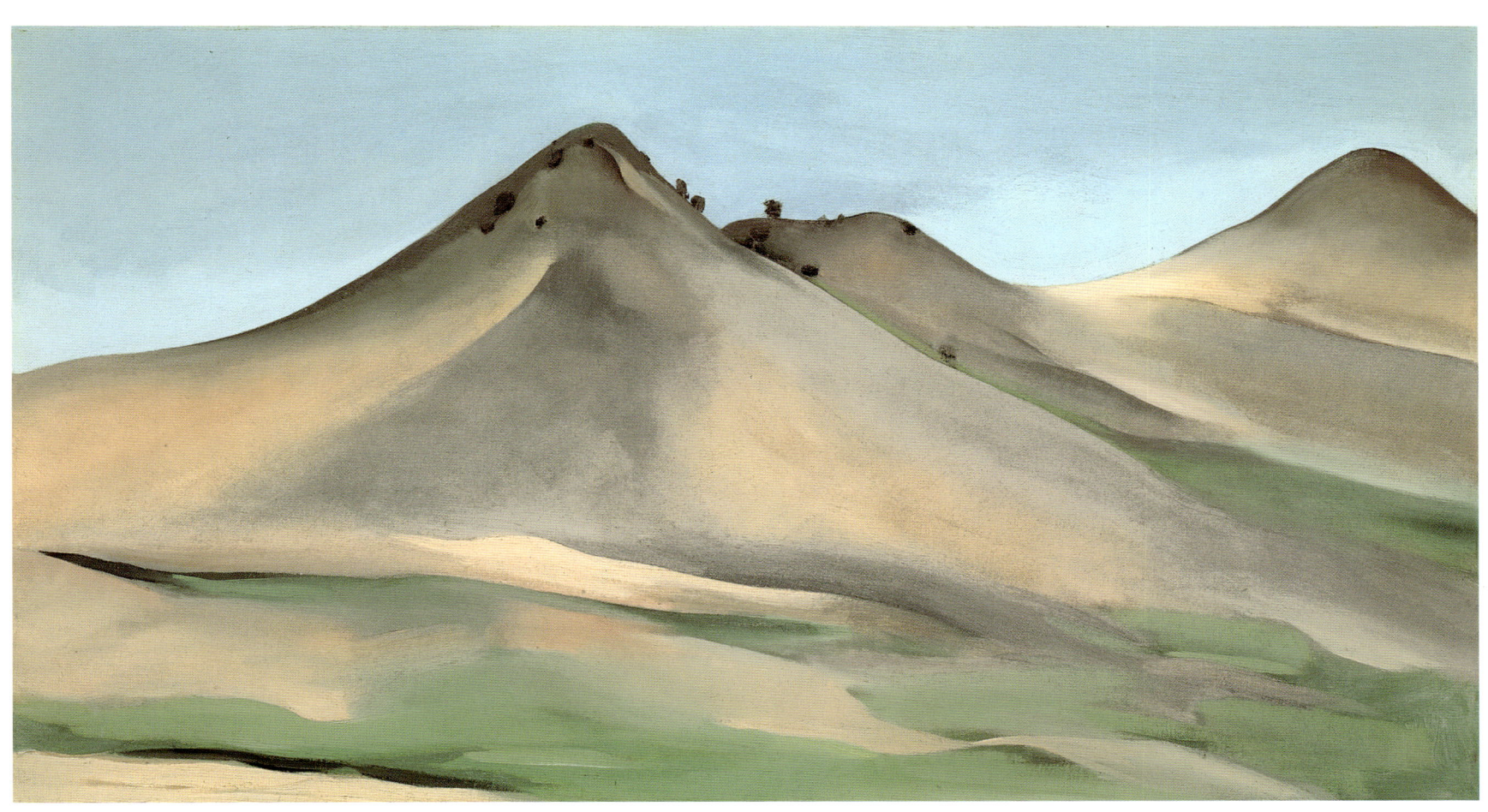

Hill, New Mexico, 1935;

The Cliff Chimneys, 1938;

Part of the Cliffs, 1937; and

Untitled (Red and Yellow Cliffs), 1940

THESE FOUR PAINTINGS are among O'Keeffe's most apparently literal depictions of the landscape forms that fascinated her at Ghost Ranch. She first discovered Ghost Ranch in 1934, and she painted the landscape forms there over the next twenty years. In *Hill, New Mexico* (plate 3), her painting of the scruffy hill and the forms adjoining it is almost identical to what is observable today (fig. 4), making this work one of O'Keeffe's most exact depictions of the natural forms to which it refers. In addition, each of the piñon and dead cedar trees documented in her painting still exists on the hill, and in fact the additional trees we see on the hill today could have been there in 1935 and been simply edited out when she made the painting.

In *The Cliff Chimneys* (plate 4), the towering chimney forms rise out of a triangular wedge of chunky orange rocks and are flanked on either side by grey-capped, irregular rocky cliffs. This configuration appears to be presented exactly as she saw it, though we cannot experience the exact view that O'Keeffe had in 1938 because a horse stable and trees that were not there when she made the painting obstruct our view. The only obvious difference between the painting and the photograph (fig. 5) seems to be that she brought the towers of the chimneys slightly closer together than they appear when viewed from the position she was in when she recorded the forms. Similarly, in *Part of the Cliffs* (plate 5), O'Keeffe more or less replicated the edges, shapes, and colors of the forms she saw, and she included the top of the craggy peaks that jut up from behind them on the left (see fig. 6).

Yet these paintings move beyond the literal. On close study, it is obvious O'Keeffe subtly manipulated the forms. In *Hill, New Mexico*, she increased the crenulations of the contours in the upper third of the hill and frosted its oddly shaped peak with thick layers of whites and greys. Furthermore, she simplified the roughly textured slopes below, creating patterns of intensified oranges and whites that read somewhere between description and abstraction. By calling attention to a few of the deep furrows that mark the surfaces of the hill, she introduced repeating and gently curving diagonals that suggest movement within the form. The hill is thus animated, seeming to be in the process of turning slowly up and out of the earth and swelling forward into the viewer's space as its crest almost meets the top edge of the painting.

Similarly, in *The Cliff Chimneys*, she slightly altered the contours of forms in both the middle ground and background, and perhaps most important, she framed the scene in order to crop the top of the right chimney—a device that calls attention to the edge of the painting and thus brings this distant form into direct contact with the planarity of the painting's surface. Too, in this painting as well as in *Part of the Cliffs* and *Untitled (Red and Yellow Cliffs)* (plate 6), O'Keeffe's interest in using color to emphasize the rhythms of repeating shapes within the boundaries of contours is even more pronounced. In *The Cliff Chimneys* there is a greatly intensified orange inverted triangle in the lower half of the painting that mirrors the similarly intensified orange triangle that appears to support the chimneys. And in *Part of the Cliffs* and *Untitled (Red and Yellow Cliffs)* orange and pink wedgelike depressions are outlined with broad bands of greyish pink, creating a series of interlocking triangular forms that read as both solids and voids. Finally, the alternating lighter and darker yellows of the forms that crown the cliffs both suggest and deny their volume, as does O'Keeffe's treatment of the thick greyish-white stratum above them. The upper parts of the cliffs seem to press down on those below them, which, curiously, appear to be as concave as they are convex. Such ambiguities between two- and three-dimensional elements create visual tensions that activate and enliven O'Keeffe's painting.

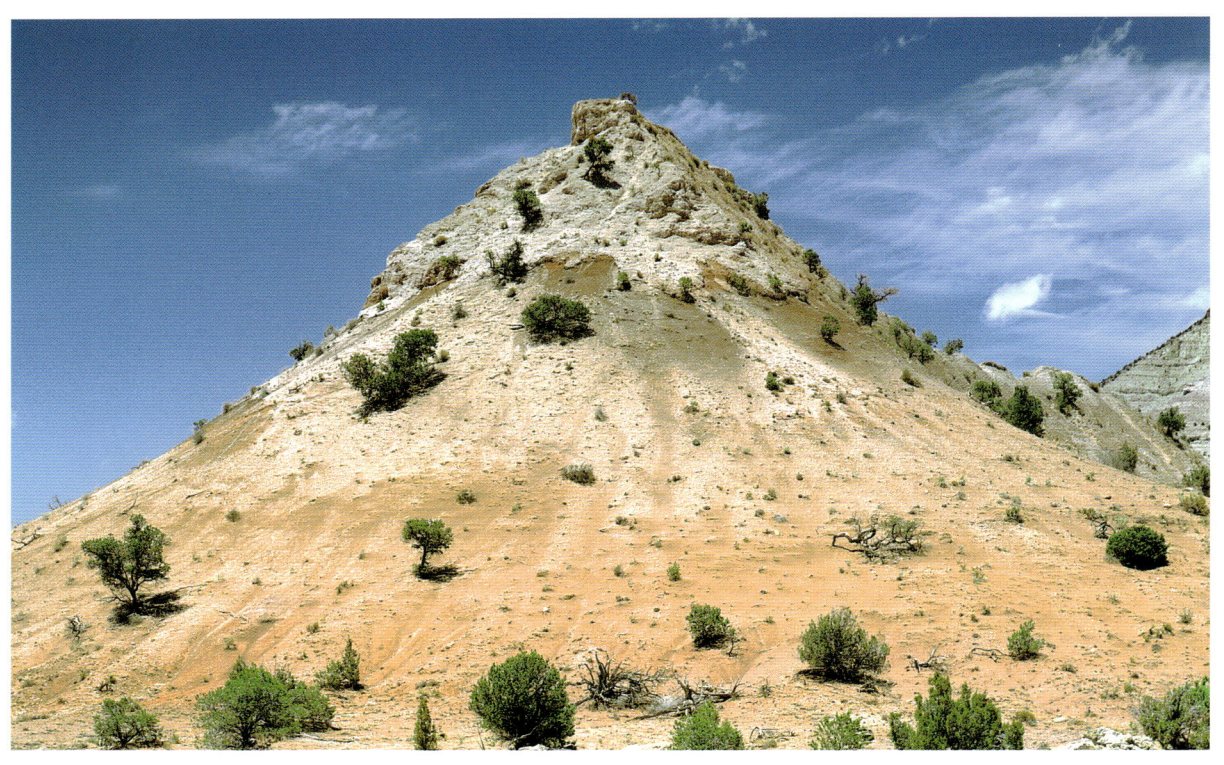

ABOVE, FIG. 4
Photograph of site of
Hill, New Mexico (plate 3)

OPPOSITE, PLATE 3
Hill, New Mexico, 1935
Oil on canvas
30 x 40 in. (76.2 x 101.6 cm)
Private collection
CR 872

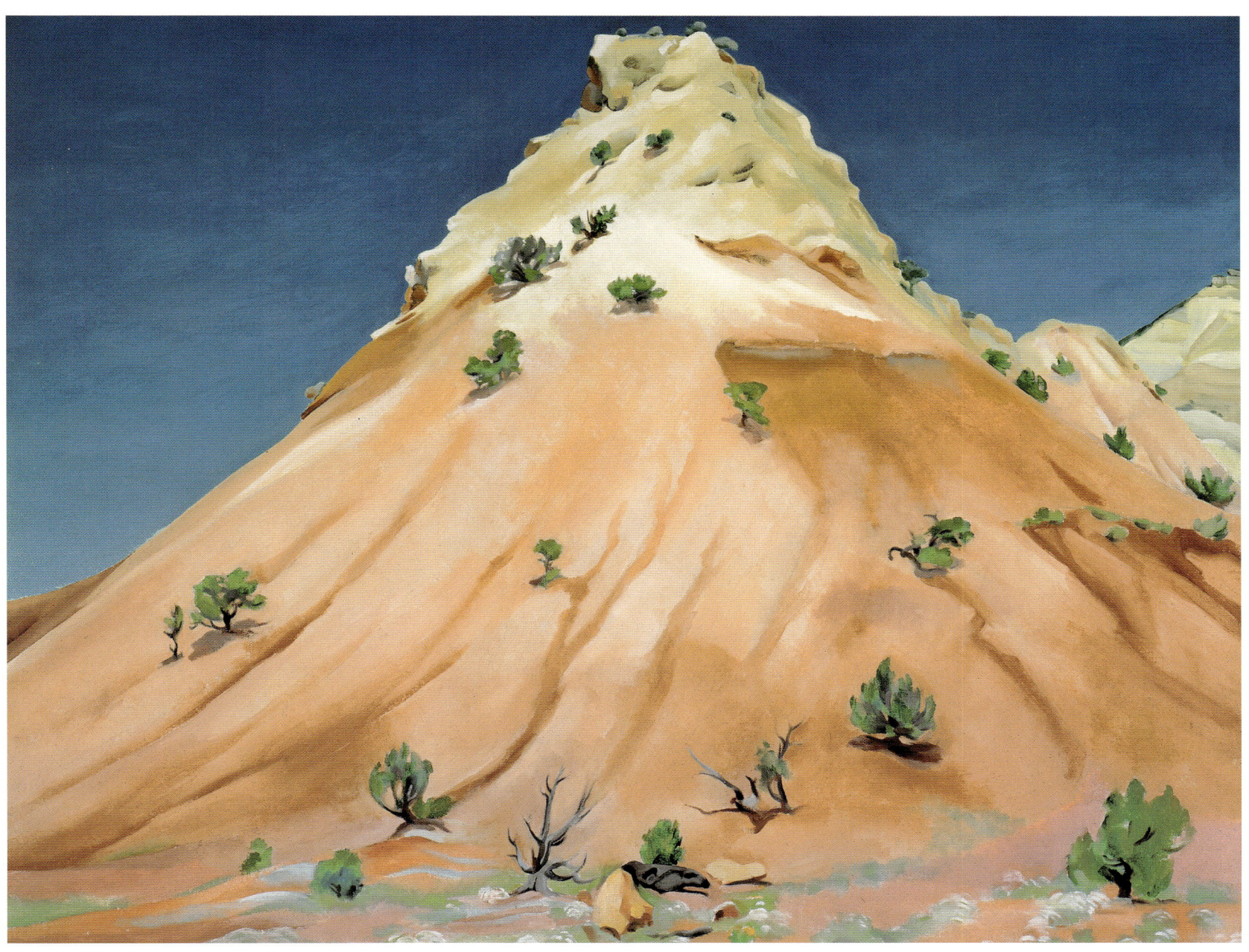

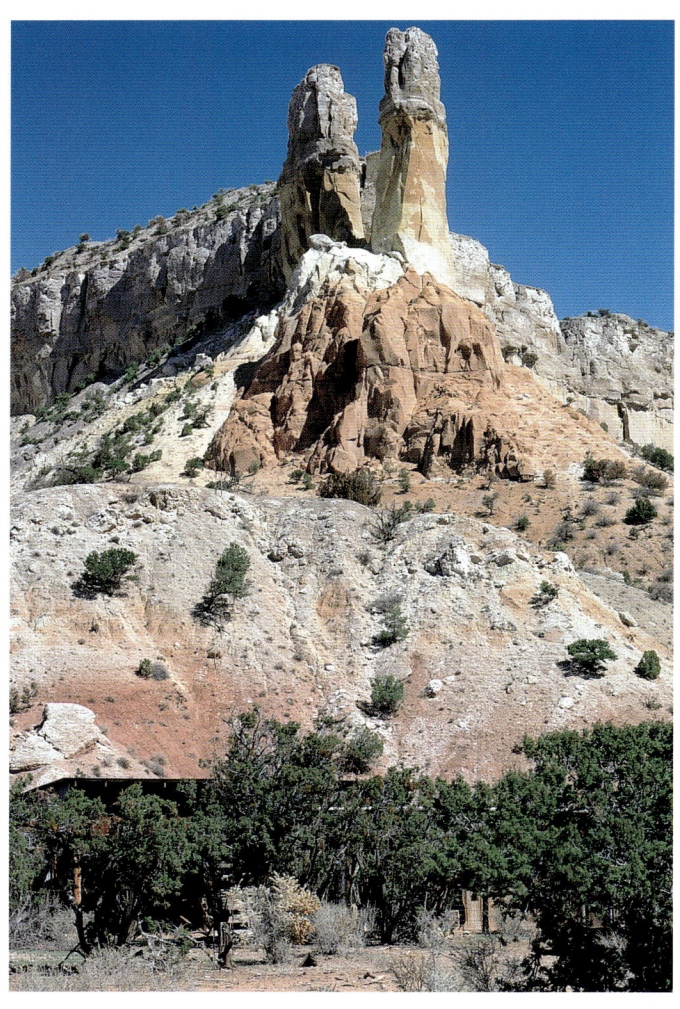

LEFT, FIG. 5
Photograph of site of
The Cliff Chimneys (plate 4)

OPPOSITE, PLATE 4
The Cliff Chimneys, 1938
Oil on canvas
36 x 30 in. (91.4 x 76.2 cm)
Milwaukee Art Museum. Gift of
Jane Bradley Pettit Foundation
and The Georgia O'Keeffe
Foundation
CR 955

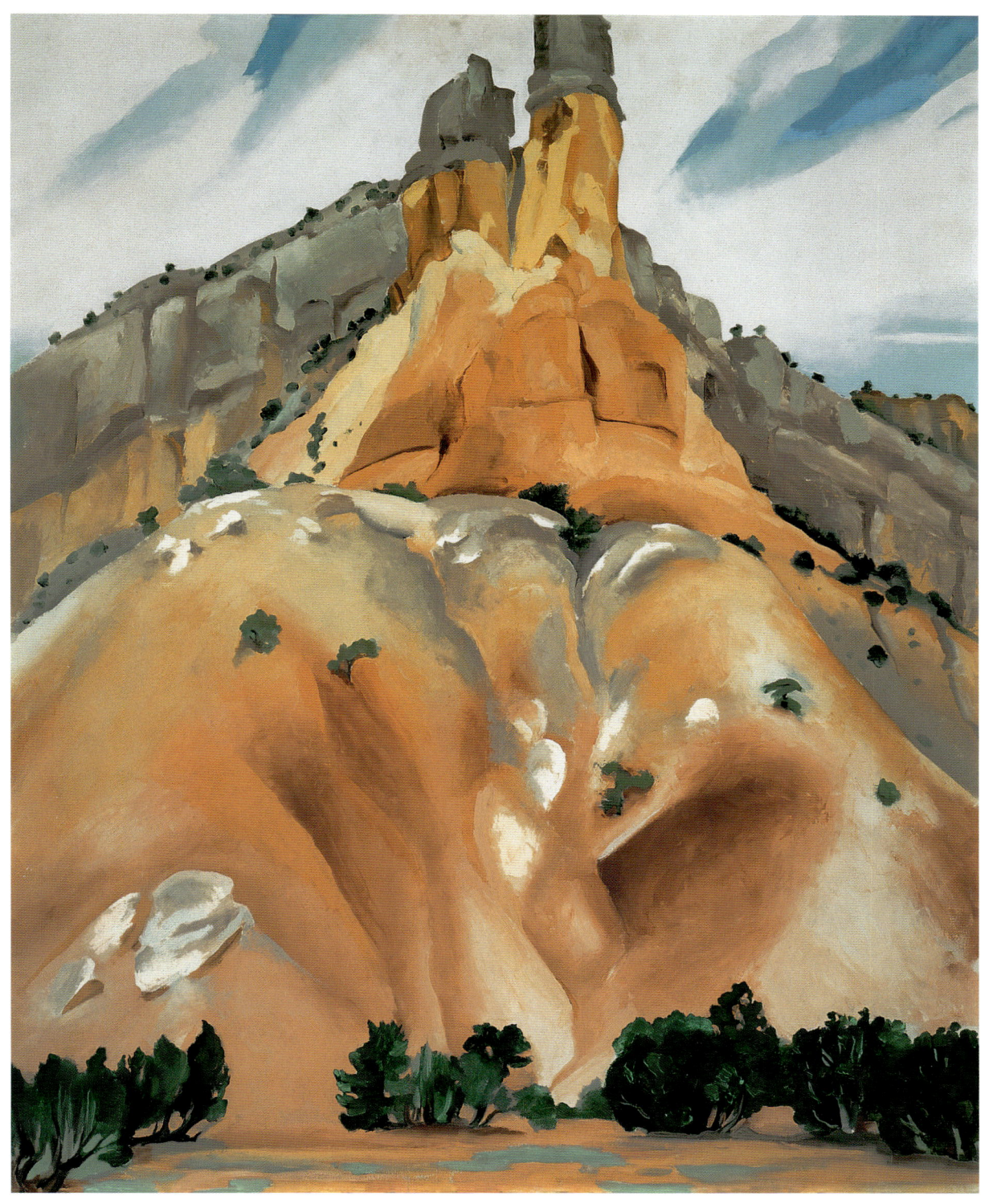

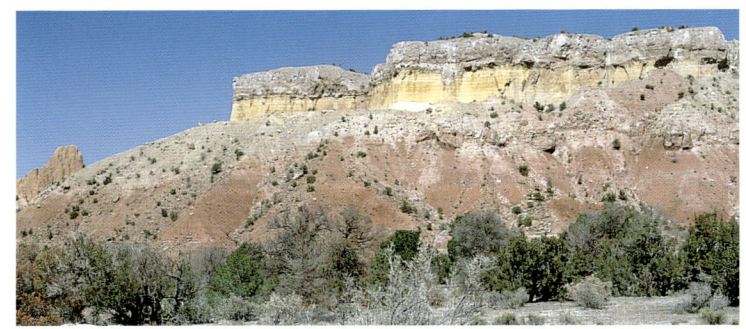

ABOVE, FIG. 6
Photograph of site of *Part of the Cliffs* and *Untitled (Red and Yellow Cliffs)* (plates 5, 6)

RIGHT, PLATE 5
Part of the Cliffs, 1937
Oil on canvas
20 x 32 in. (50.8 x 81.3 cm)
Private collection
CR 931

OPPOSITE, PLATE 6
Untitled (Red and Yellow Cliffs),
1940
Oil on canvas
24 x 36 in. (61 x 91.4 cm)
Georgia O'Keeffe Museum,
Santa Fe, N. Mex. Gift of The
Burnett Foundation
CR 998

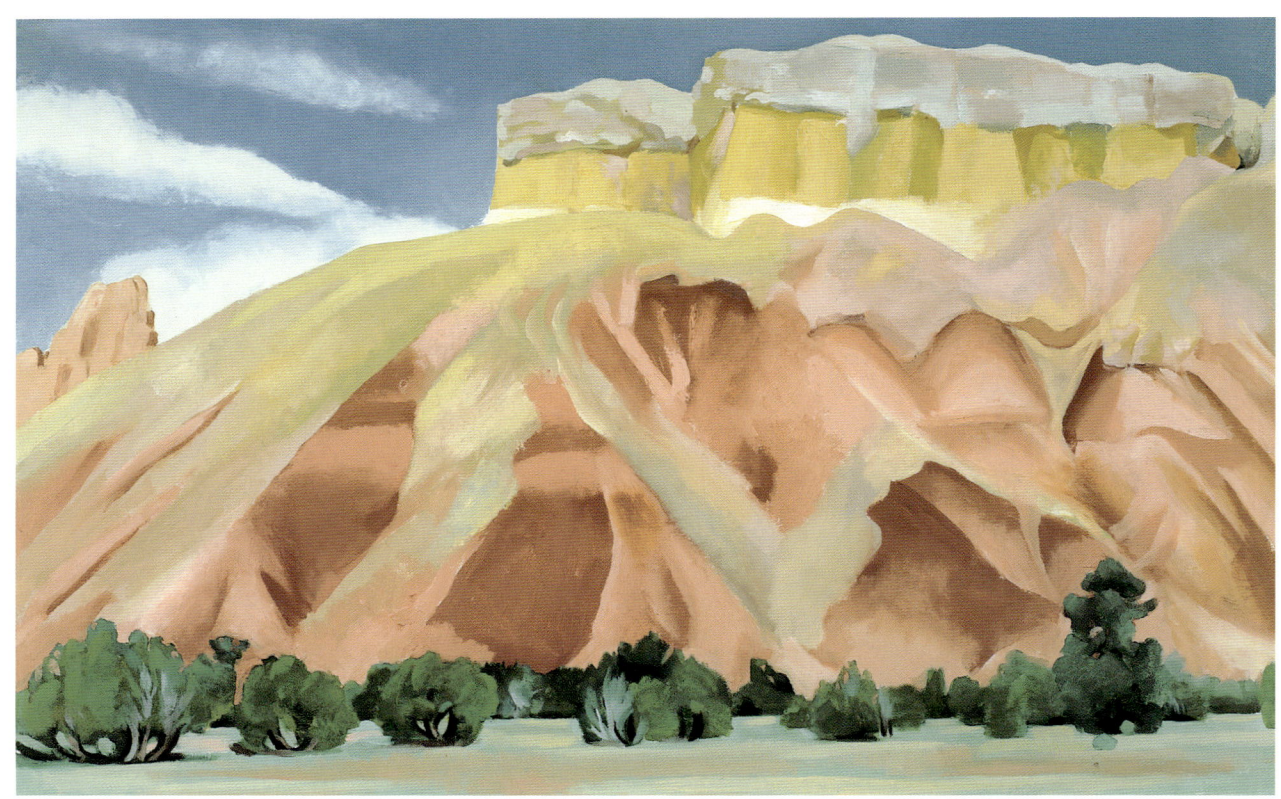

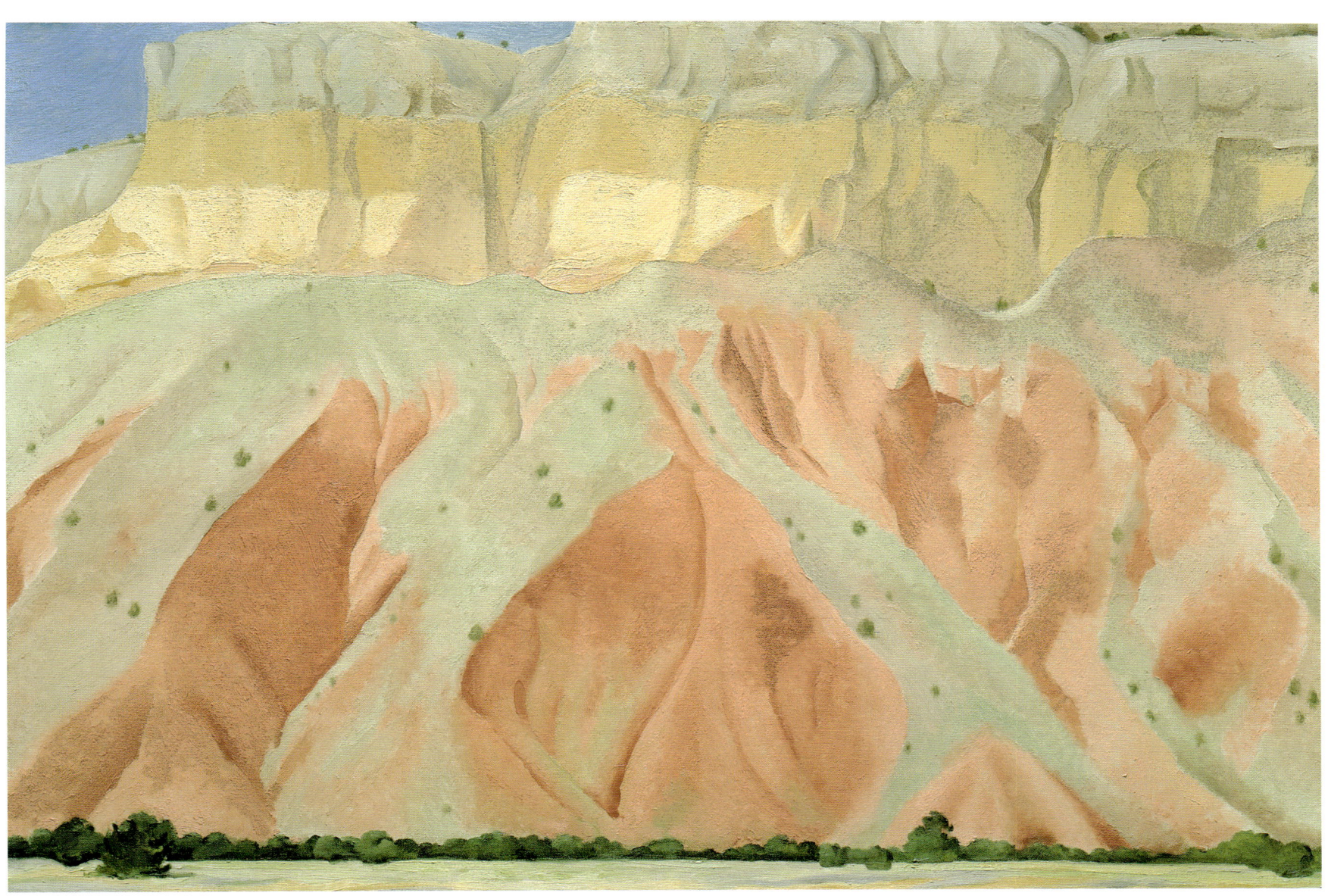

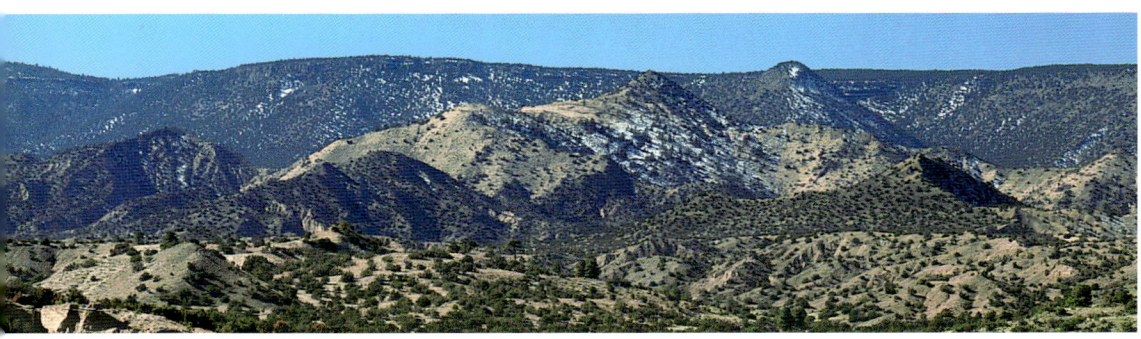

THESE TWO PAINTINGS (plates 7 and 8) have identical subjects. To reach this landscape configuration (fig. 7), O'Keeffe drove west in the Tierra Azul area and walked toward it. In both paintings, she used a thin band of blue sky and the gently undulating horizontal of the top of the dark mesa just below it to isolate a specific area of hills to the left and right of the area's two most distinctive peaks. She positioned herself so that one of the peaks rose to touch the contour of the mesa and one rose above it.

In both compositions the overall placement of the repeating hill forms is much as it appears in the actual landscape, but O'Keeffe made subtle changes in their relationships. She also omitted any references to the trees that cover them, limiting the occurrence of vegetation to a line of green along the bottom edge of *Near Abiquiu, N.M. 2*. The omission of vegetation from the hills permitted her to reveal the underlying structure of the landscape—which is not at all apparent in the photograph.

In *Near Abiquiu, N.M. 2*, as the denuded contours of the hill forms rise and fall within the framework of two strong horizontals—the edge of the mesa and the line of trees at the bottom of the composition—they create dynamic linear rhythms that do not occur in the actual forms in the landscape and thus are unrelated to this subject's overwhelming stasis and solidity. O'Keeffe amplified these movements in *Near Abiquiu, New Mexico*. She narrowed her focus by cropping the view on the right, eliminating the trees in the foreground, and compressing and simplifying the

ABOVE, FIG. 7
Photograph of site of *Near Abiquiu, N.M. 2* and *Near Abiquiu, New Mexico* (plates 7, 8)

OPPOSITE, PLATE 7
Near Abiquiu, N.M. 2, 1930
Oil on canvas
10 x 24⅛ in. (25.4 x 61.3 cm)
The Metropolitan Museum of Art, New York. Alfred Stieglitz Collection, 1963 (63.204)
CR 735

shapes. With the exception of the blue of the sky, all the colors are intensified, with the darks becoming richer and the yellow hills moving more toward a soft salmon. With its strong linear accents and invented dark elements denying the intrinsic volume of the hills, this painting takes on a planarity not evident in the earlier one. Through these manipulations, O'Keeffe transformed what she saw into what is essentially an abstraction that presents a series of interrelated forms as if seen close up or through a telephoto lens. In so doing, she employed a device—magnification—that she had used in earlier work, especially in her large-scale views of flowers.

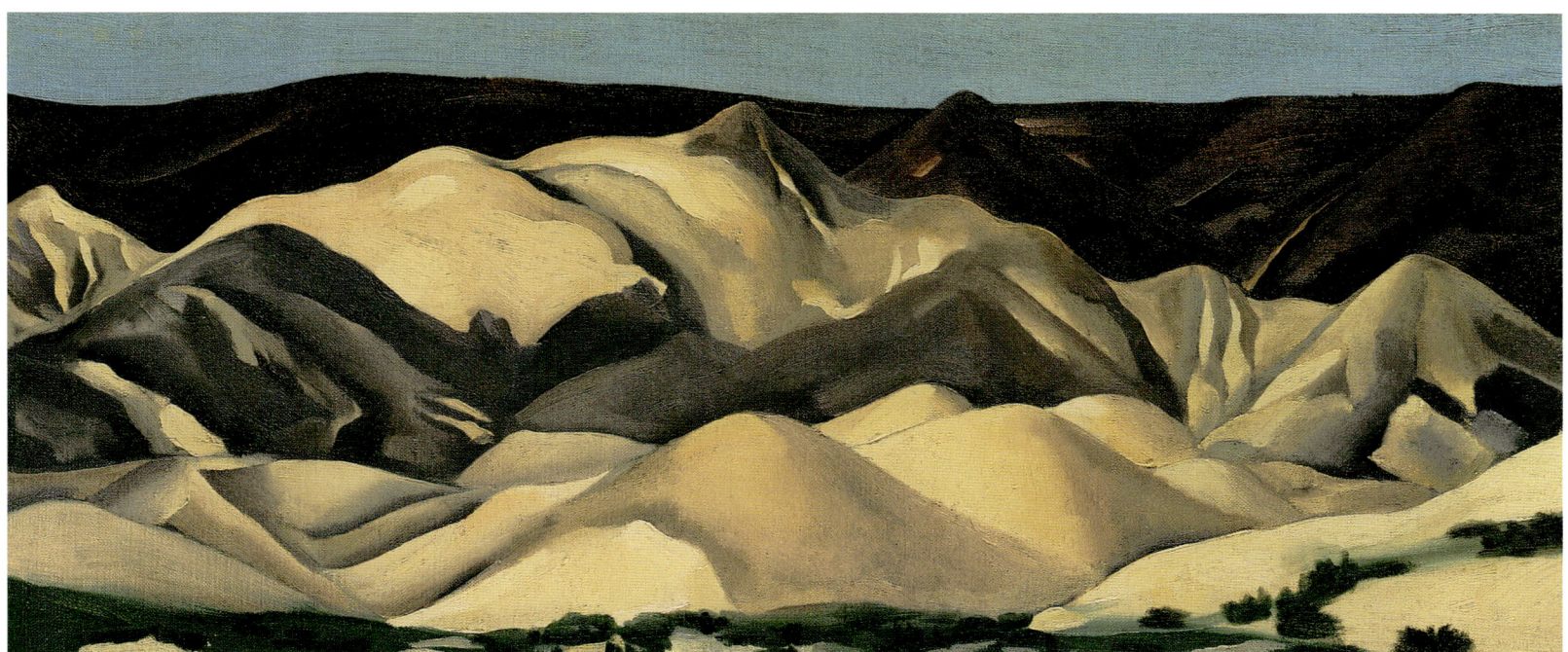

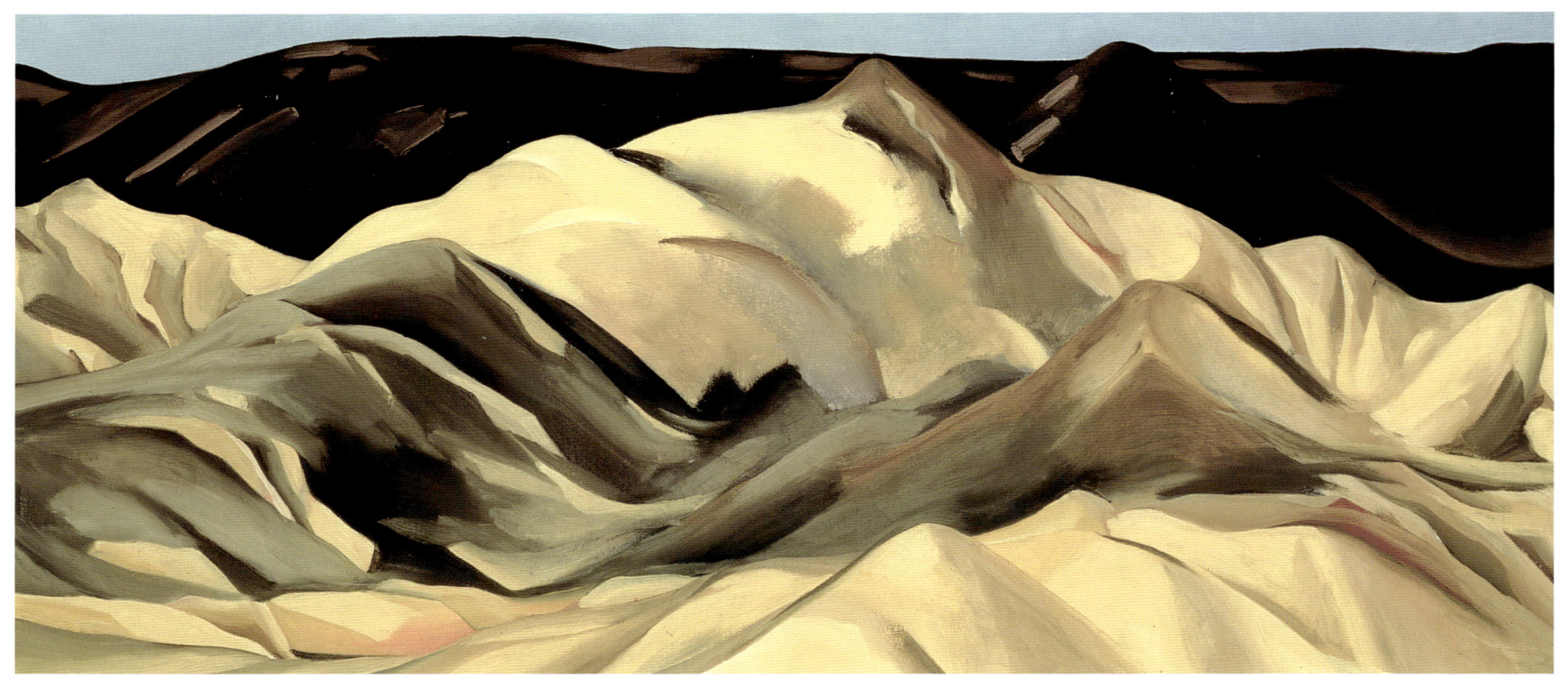

PLATE 8
Near Abiquiu, New Mexico, 1931
Oil on canvas
16 x 36 in. (40.6 x 91.4 cm)
Private collection
CR 794

NEW MEXICO LANDSCAPE, MESA WITH LOW HILLS, 1930;

LAVENDER HILL FORMS, 1934;

PURPLE HILLS GHOST RANCH—2 / PURPLE HILLS NO. II, 1934;

CEDAR TREE WITH LAVENDER HILLS, 1937; AND *MY RED HILLS*, 1938

IN 1930 O'KEEFFE ALSO TURNED her attention to the small mesa that appears, in part, on the far right of *Near Abiquiu, N.M. 2* (plate 7). In *New Mexico Landscape, Mesa with Low Hills* (plate 9), she replicated the overall shape and major internal contours of the forms, but that is the extent of this work's relationship to the actual landscape (fig. 8). She compressed the mesa into a smaller, more compact unit, intensified its blackness, and highlighted the subtle forms she saw within it with grey and, on its right, with three strokes of orange. Thus, the black mesa becomes an ominous backdrop against which the artist dramatized the dynamic interplay of the unusual triangular shapes along its base by describing them with reds, oranges, and yellows of her own invention, relating them to the mesa form with an upward thrust of orange on the extreme left and those three orange strokes. Although O'Keeffe had intensified the color in *Black Mesa Landscape, New Mexico / Out Back of Marie's II* (plate 1), the hues relate specifically to those in the landscape. Here she arbitrarily imposed colors on the forms she saw as a means of emphasizing the differences between them.

O'Keeffe was fascinated by the fact that the colors she loved and had long used in her work occurred naturally in the landscape configurations that surrounded her at Ghost Ranch. As she explained to her friend the critic Henry McBride in 1939: "Badlands roll away from my door, hill after hill—red hills of apparently the same sort of earth that you mix with oil to make paint. . . . All the earth colors of the painter's palette are out there in the many miles of badlands. The light Naples yellow through the ochres—orange and red and purple earth—even the soft earth greens."[5]

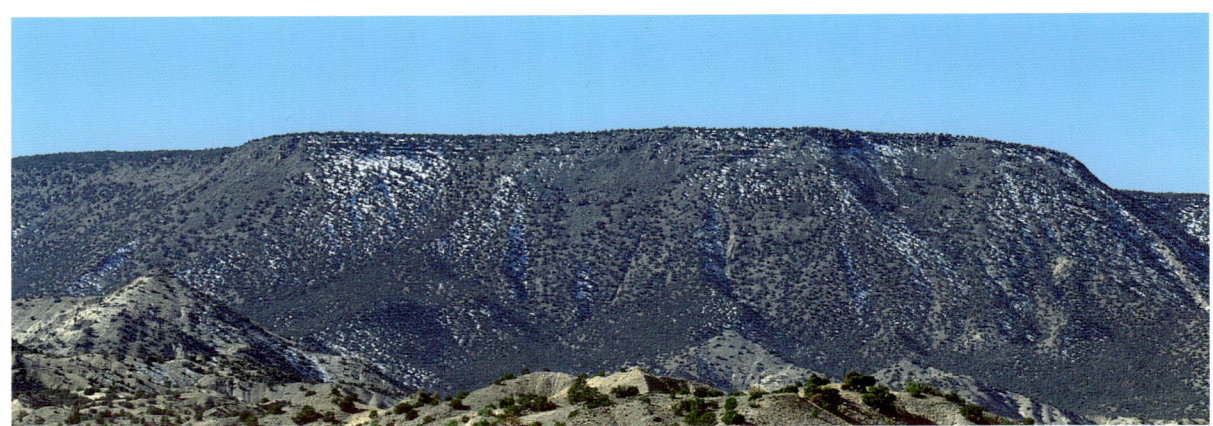

On walks among these richly colorful hills and cliffs, she observed the way the changing light affected these colors and how this altered the apparent relationships between forms. As she wrote in 1937: "I climbed way up on a pale green hill and in the evening light—the sun under the clouds—the color effect was very strange—standing high on a pale green hill where I could look all around at the red, yellow, purple formations—miles all around—the colors all intensified by the pale grey green I was standing on. It was wonderful."[6]

When O'Keeffe first began working at Ghost Ranch, she made several paintings of hills in one of its eastern ranges, including *Lavender Hill Forms* (plate 10) and *Purple Hills Ghost Ranch—2 / Purple Hills No. II* (plate 11). From a distance, the contours of and shapes within these liver-colored undulating hills are very difficult to discern because they blend into those of the hills that rise behind them. As one approaches these forms, however, the profusion of landscape elements behind them disappears, and the hills rise dramatically as a single unit against the sky, much as O'Keeffe depicted them in her paintings (see fig. 9).

Deep furrows run from the top to the bottom of these hills and create linear patterns on their roughly textured surfaces. In one stratum of the hills, sections have eroded to form a horizontal line of gaping holes, and two sets of low, undulating hills rise along their bases. In *Purple Hills Ghost*

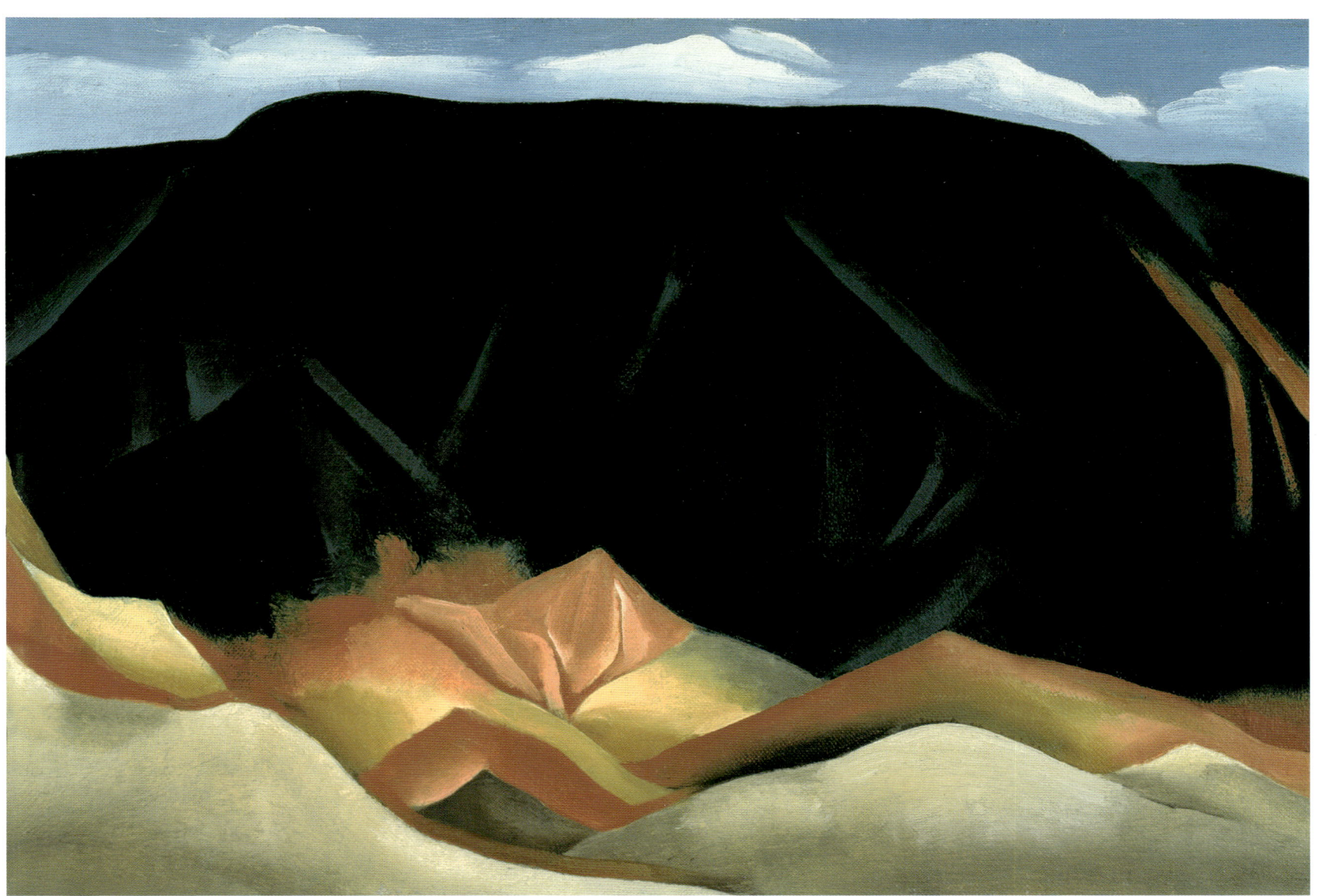

Ranch—2 / Purple Hills No. II, O'Keeffe presented the lower and upper areas of hills as two nearly equal components of the composition. The actual contours of these forms correspond generally to those that appear in her paintings of them, but her manipulations within the contours are obvious.

She exaggerated the protrusions she observed in the hill, and in her painting the one at the center becomes much larger and more dynamic. She used the natural colors—rust browns, earth greens, and dull pinks—as a point of departure, but the painting also has intensified pinks, oranges, lavenders, and greens applied in long, even strokes that ignore the actual surface texture of the forms at the same time they suggest an interplay between the forms and deny their volumes. The colorful abstract patterns are recognizable as a landscape primarily because of O'Keeffe's relative faithfulness to its primary contours.

The horizontal line of deep gouges so evident in the photograph of these hills (fig. 9) is referred to in a token way in *Purple Hills Ghost Ranch—2 / Purple Hills No. II*. In *Lavender Hill Forms* the gouges are one of the most dynamic elements in the composition, appearing as triangular openings in the hill. Some are filled with intense oranges and capped with purple, and O'Keeffe wittily highlighted the area above each with a curved white line, which in some cases resembles an eyebrow above a half-closed eye. This painting also presents a more narrowly focused view of the hills, and their contours rise and fall far more dramatically, as if the hills have been compressed horizontally.

But *Lavender Hill Forms* is perhaps most inventive in its palette. O'Keeffe seems to have used most of the colors she saw in the overall landscape at Ghost Ranch, but invented most of the colors she used in this specific painting. By synthesizing the great variety of hues that could be seen at Ghost Ranch at various times of day, depending on the light, she created a Fauve-like vision of a subject whose actual color can only be characterized as subtle.

When O'Keeffe returned to these hills in 1937 to paint a dead cedar tree in front of them (plate 12), she used them as an elaborate stage set to showcase a single form. As earlier, she took

OPPOSITE, PLATE 10

Lavender Hill Forms, 1934

Oil on canvas

16 x 30 in. (40.6 x 76.2 cm)

Private collection

CR 836

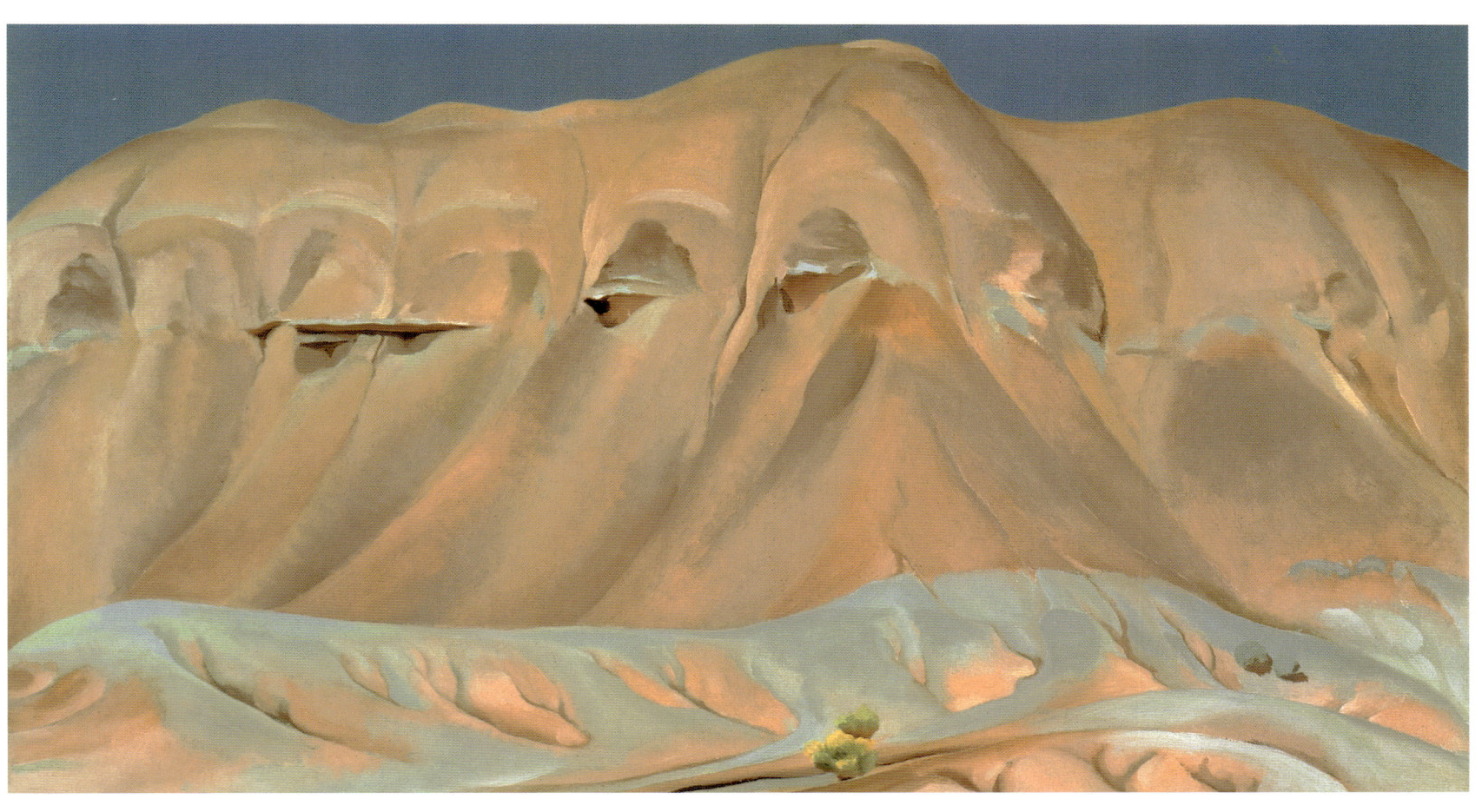

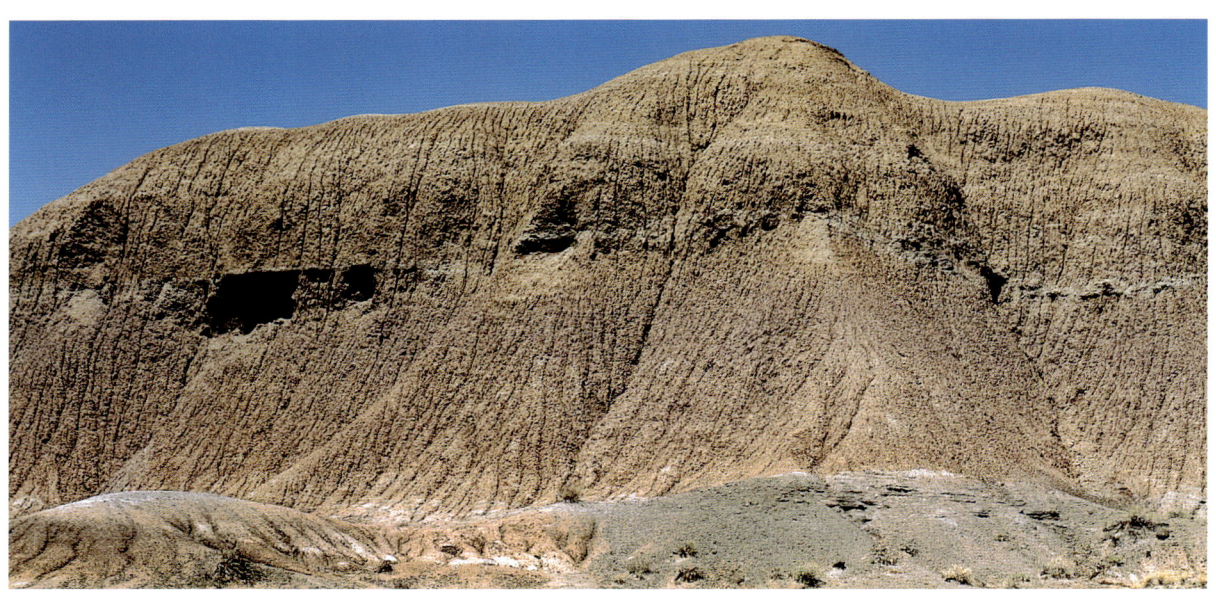

great liberties with the color and shapes of the hills and surrounding landscape, but curiously, she described both the tree's form and its color rather specifically. All of the forms depicted in *Cedar Tree with Lavender Hills* still exist (fig. 10), but the piñon trees have grown taller and multiplied. And even though O'Keeffe may have slightly elongated the lower half of the tree's trunk, she replicated its overall shape in a remarkably faithful way.

The way she described the ground plane around the tree and the background, however, has little or nothing to do with what she saw. The interlocking pattern of pale green, grey-blue, and orange-pink she invented in the foreground relates directly to the similar, if more intense, colors she used in the background right up to the horizon. The purple hills are amorphous shapes to the left of the tree and are recognizable to the right of the tree only by O'Keeffe's inclusion of their horizontal band of depressions. The result is a composition in which a rather precise rendering of a tree exists within a highly abstracted landscape in which spatial recession is suggested only by the relative size of the piñon trees halfway up the composition. Because of these contradictions between two- and

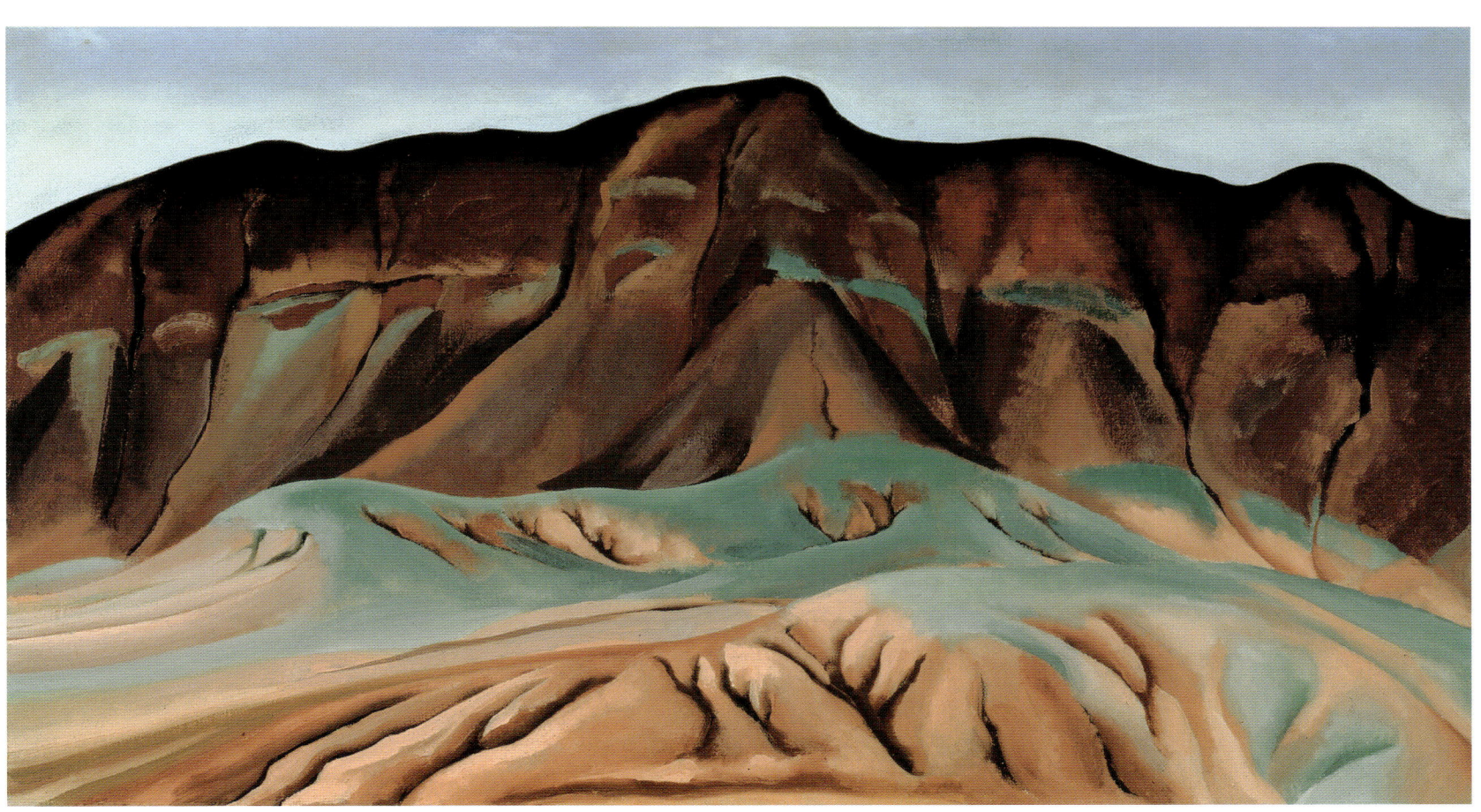

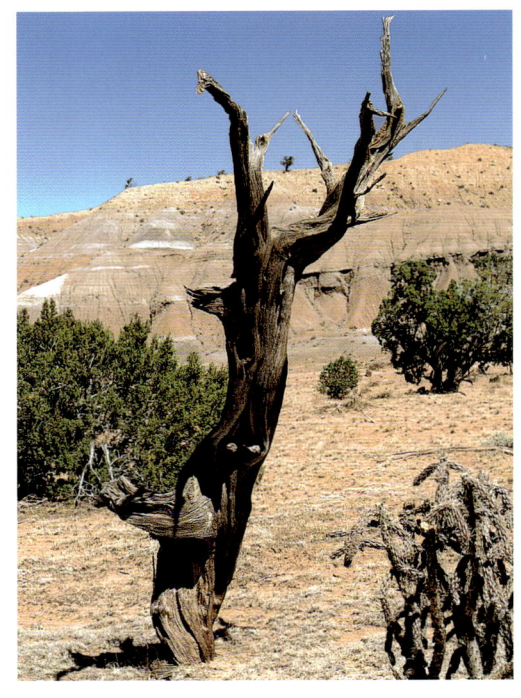

three-dimensional pictorial elements, there is an enormous tension in the painting that is not present in the actual landscape.

O'Keeffe's suggestion of a short shadow cast by the tree from left to right (more or less west to east) implies the painting was made in the early afternoon. Yet the tree is also lighted from the front, and indeed, particular components, such as the knot along its trunk and the oval crevice toward its base, from which two egglike shapes protrude, are clearly visible only in the early morning, when the sun shines directly on the tree from the right. Thus the tree seems to have been presented as it appeared at various times of day, lending it a timeless quality that underscores O'Keeffe's invention.

The following year, in *My Red Hills* (plate 13), O'Keeffe created an equally imaginative work whose title claimed an area of the badlands as her own. Here she experimented once again

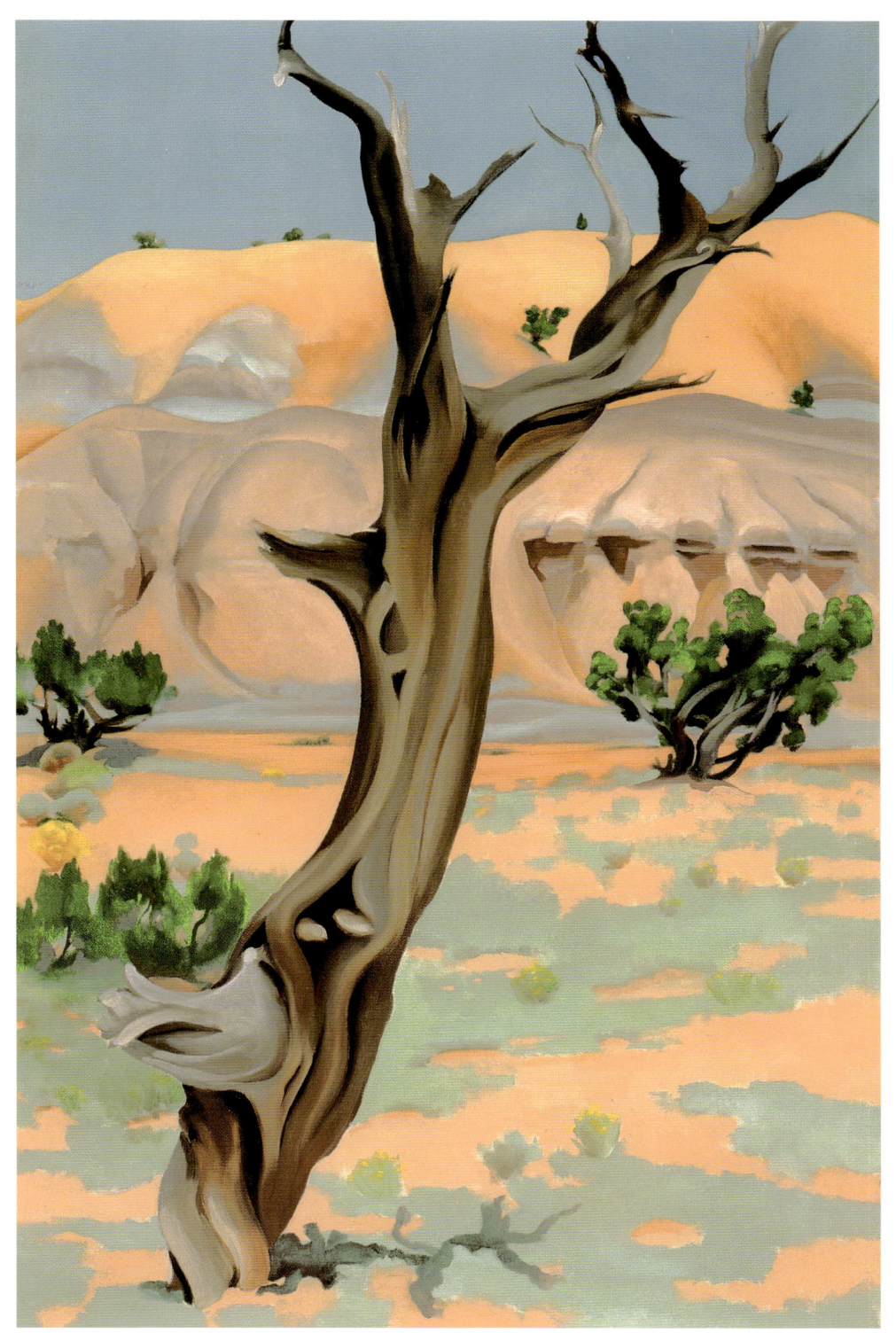

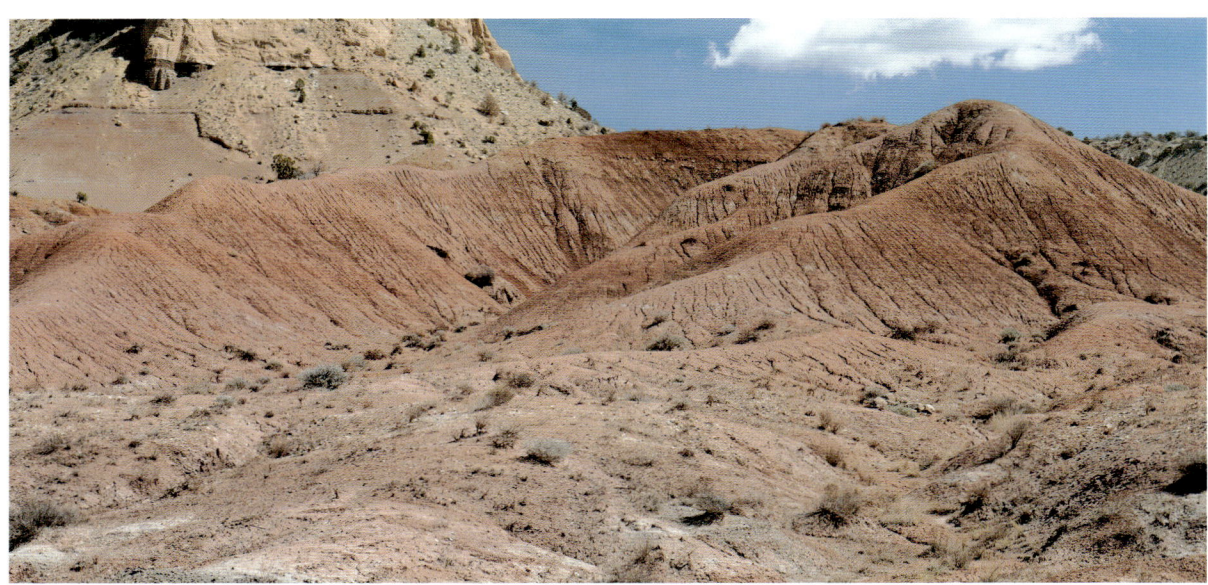

with the selective isolation of a relatively small section of the landscape, with extreme spatial compression, and with the drama that can be achieved with highly intensified, almost monochromatic color. It is clear from the photograph of the site (fig. 11) that the painting compresses the hill forms into a space that suggests no relationship to anything outside itself and seems barely able to contain the profusion of undulating shapes. The fact that this painting has no reference to the sky increases the intentional effect of airlessness.

The photograph documents the configuration of the hills that pile up around and inside one another on the right side of the painting. What it does not document are the two receding ridges of hills that appear at the painting's upper left. These forms occur in the landscape but can only be seen by climbing to the top of a nearby hill and looking down on this cluster of red hills from an entirely different perspective. Thus, to convey the full range of her experience of this complex of rhythmic shapes, O'Keeffe synthesized two points of view into one painting.

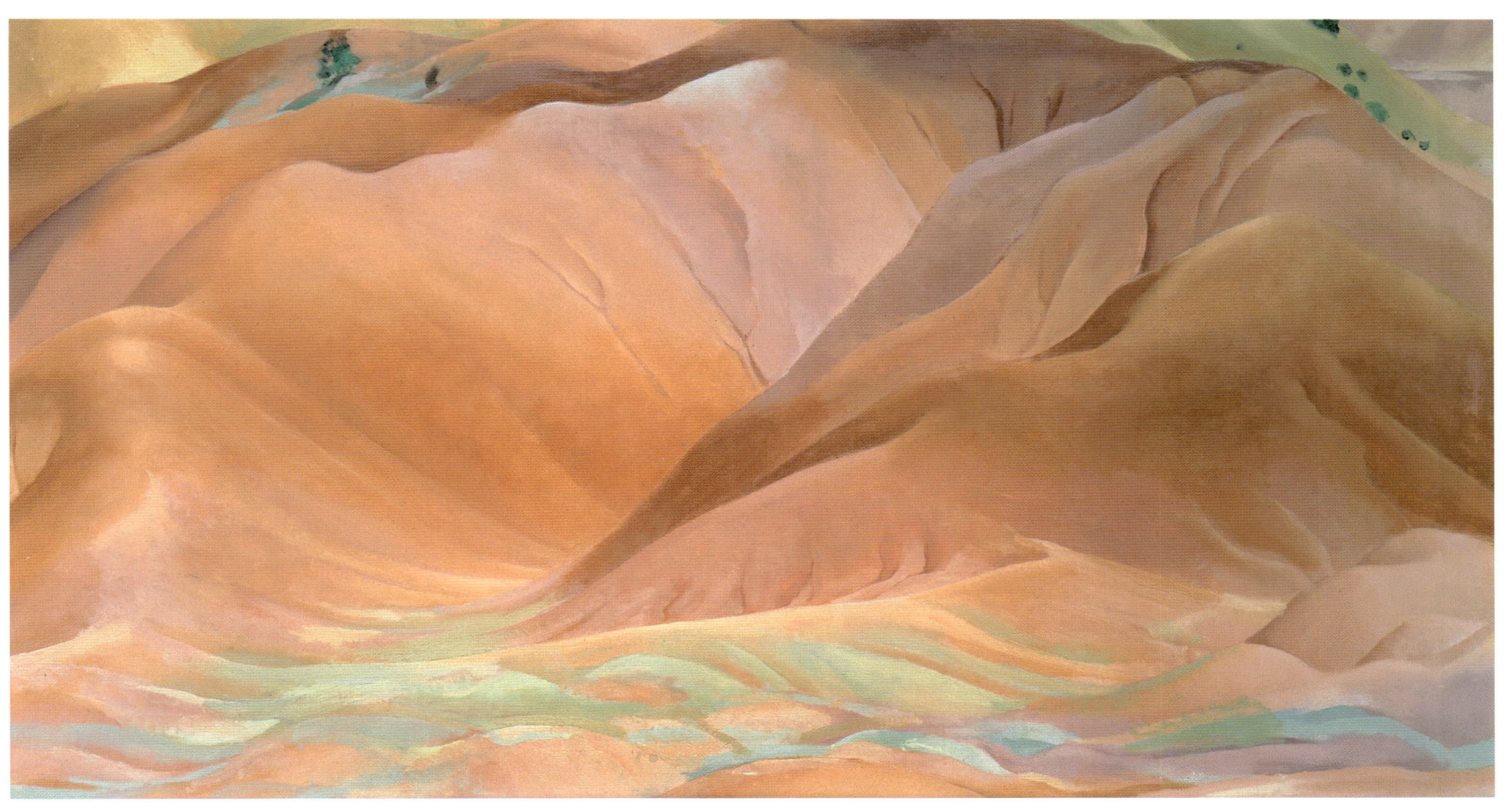

FROM THE WHITE PLACE, 1940;

WHITE PLACE IN SHADOW, 1941;

GREY HILLS, 1941; AND

BLACK PLACE III, 1944

IN THE 1940S O'KEEFFE BEGAN DEPICTING the enormous white cliffs in the Plaza Colorado, a land grant north of Abiquiu. Her paintings of these extraordinary landscape forms—which she called the White Place—in many ways replicate their actual shapes, and in painting the two massive cliff forms on the left and right sides of the composition, she used a rather traditional modulation of lights and darks to define one cliff as concave and the other as convex. At the same time, however, she used color—subtle greens, whites, yellows, and greys—to define the deep space of the canyon between the cliffs. But because these areas of color also read as relatively flat shapes in *From The White Place* (plate 14) and advance because of their chromatism, they deny any recession into depth, just as the opaque grey form at the bottom of the canyon blocks both the view into the canyon and, in fact, visual access to it from the ground.

O'Keeffe synthesized two points of view in this painting. The cliff on the right is seen from slightly below and to the left—a point of view closely resembled by the photograph (fig. 12). The left cliff is

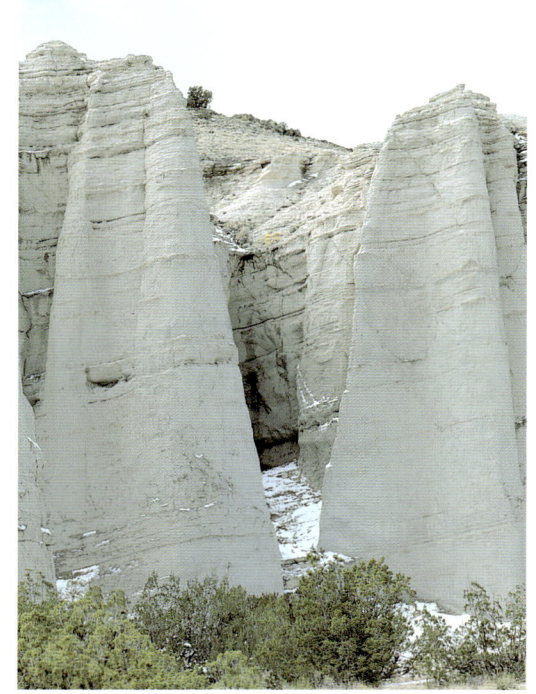

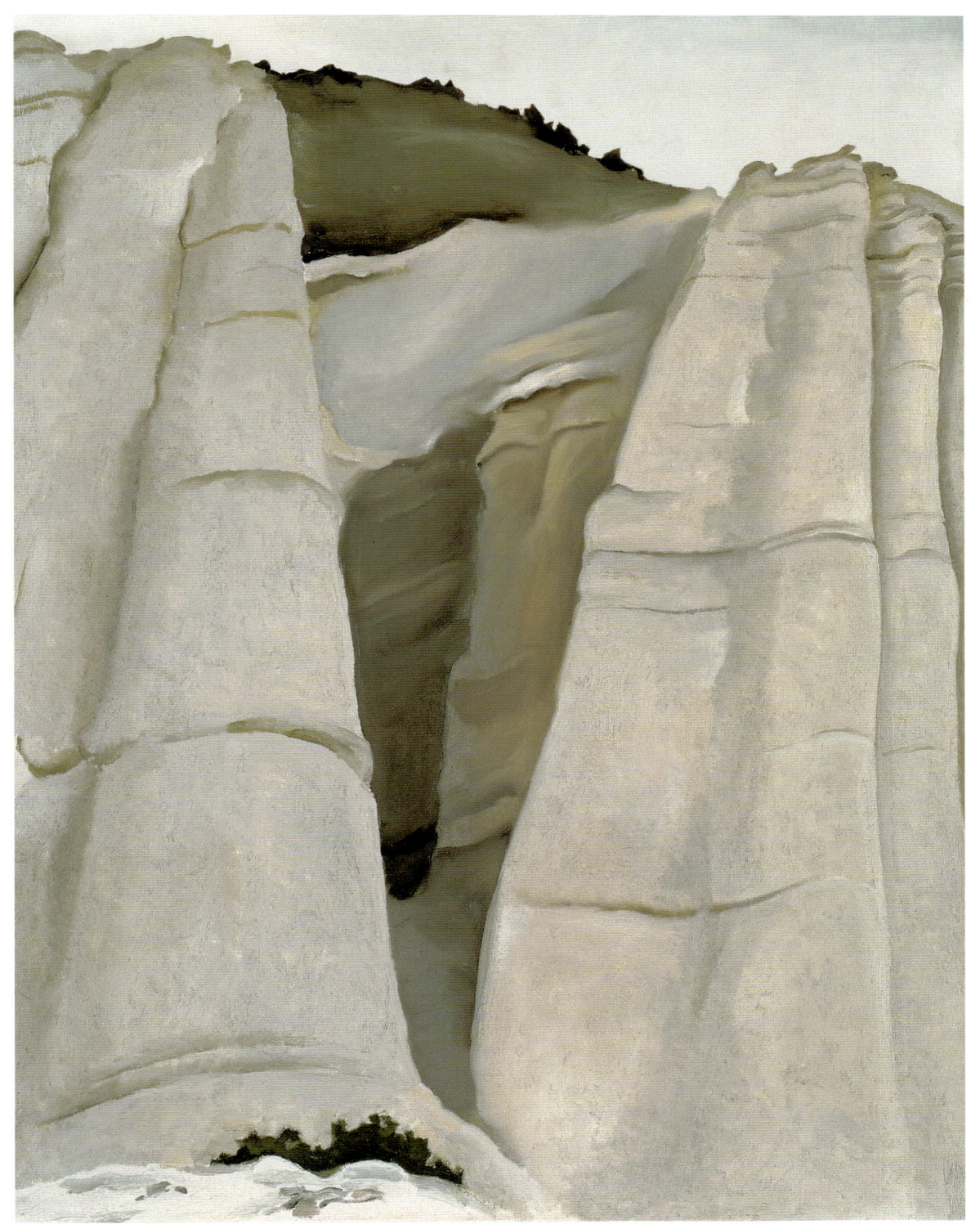

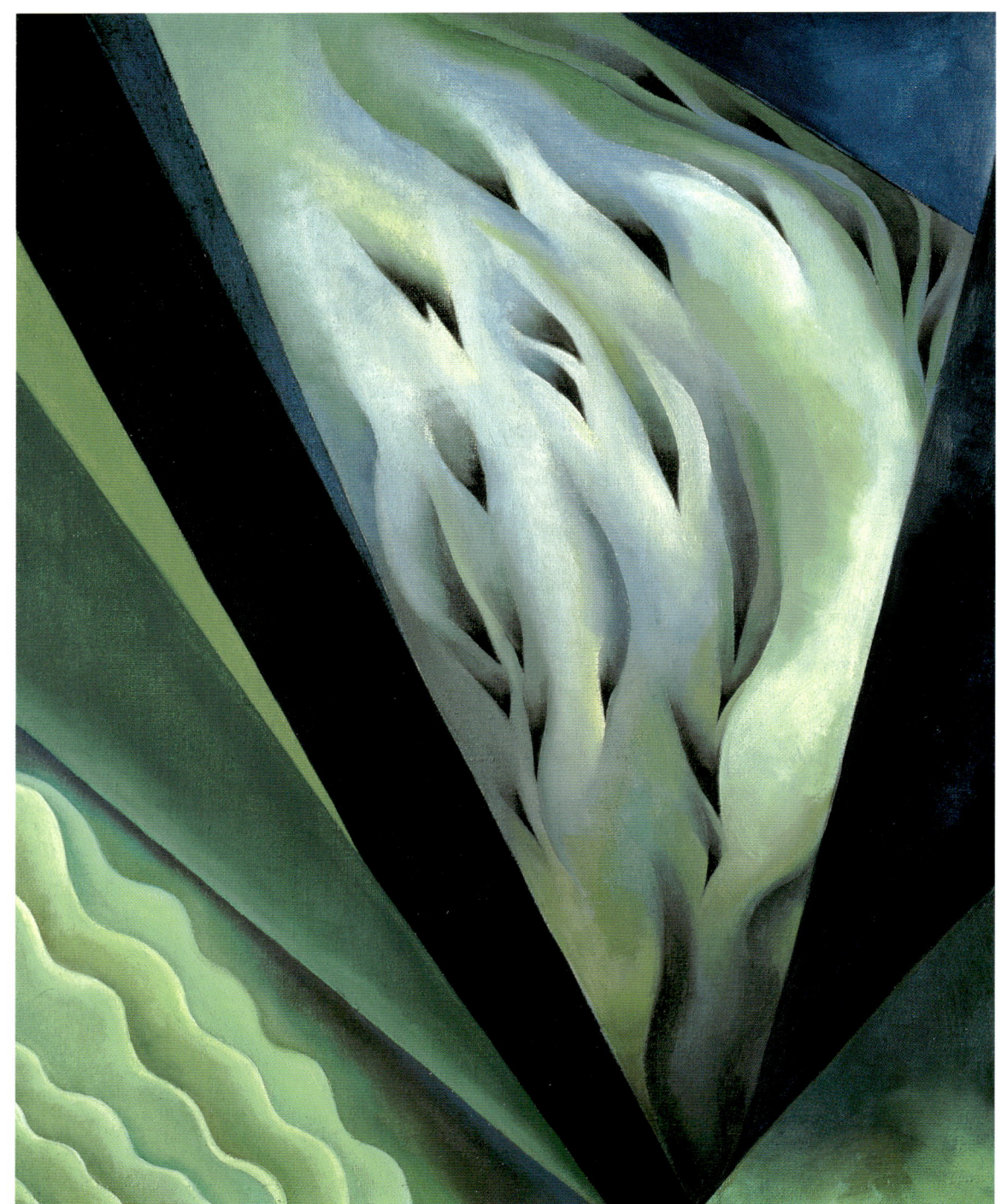

FIG. 13
Blue and Green Music, 1921
Oil on canvas
23 x 19 in. (58.4 x 48.3 cm)
The Art Institute of Chicago.
Alfred Stieglitz Collection.
Gift of Georgia O'Keeffe
(1969.835)
CR 344

seen from a point much lower and farther to the right. O'Keeffe changed the shape of the base of this form so that it meets the base of the cliff on the right, whose contours swell out and into the opening between them, thus further closing off access to the canyon.

Using these devices, O'Keeffe emphasized the V-shape of the canyon's entrance, a shape that had interested her since 1915, when she completed abstractions such as *No. 9 Special* (The Menil Collection, Houston), and which she further explored in paintings of the 1920s, such as *Blue and Green Music* (fig. 13).[7] Having discovered this much-loved form occurring as a natural component of the White Place landscape, she explored it in several other paintings that also appear to be accurate depictions of recognizable elements in the landscape.

In *White Place in Shadow* (plate 15), painted a year after *From The White Place*, O'Keeffe focused more specifically on another and more dramatic V-shape in this landscape configuration. The contours in this painting are a remarkably literal translation of those seen in the photograph (fig. 14). The inverted T-shape included near the bottom of the painting derives from a shape that can be seen near the base of the cleft. Indeed, the greater literalness of this picture suggests a reversal in O'Keeffe's usual habit of working in series from the specific to the abstract.

Yet, primarily because of her extreme cropping in this painting, the white cliffs function less as subject than as frame, isolating a large shape of blue sky that seems to be suspended from the top and upper-left edges. Although very subtly modulated from top to bottom, the blue functions as an advancing element in the composition and, combined with a simple system of overlapping planes in the cliff forms, contributes to the overall denial of spatial recession in this work.

O'Keeffe's interest in the nearby White Place was eclipsed by her interest in a group of low, dark hills in a desolate area, some 150 miles west of Ghost Ranch, that she called the Black Place and to which she kept returning to paint over a thirteen-year period. *Grey Hills* (plate 16) was made at the Black Place, and the photograph of the specific site was made from her exact vantage point (fig. 15). Although the contours and forms of the rugged black hills documented in the photograph do appear in the painting, O'Keeffe compressed her subject into a configuration that seems more densely vertical than the photograph indicates. Again she took her palette from the scene at hand, but there is far more color modulation in the painting than is apparent in the photograph. Nonetheless, *Grey Hills* is a relatively faithful record of what can be seen at the site. When O'Keeffe returned to these black hills later in the 1940s, she increasingly used them as a framework for abstraction, often making certain motifs, like V- and zigzag shapes, the dominant elements in her compositions. One resulting painting, *Black Place III* (plate 17), is among the most accomplished of her landscape abstractions. It bears little relationship to a specific site in the northwestern New Mexico landscape; rather, it is a synthesis of forms that may have been extracted from several sites and then filtered through years of seeking to summarize, not specify, visual experience.

RIGHT, FIG. 14
Photograph of site of
White Place in Shadow
(plate 15)

OPPOSITE, PLATE 15
White Place in Shadow, 1941
Oil on canvas
19 x 10 in. (48.3 x 25.4 cm)
Private collection
CR 1027

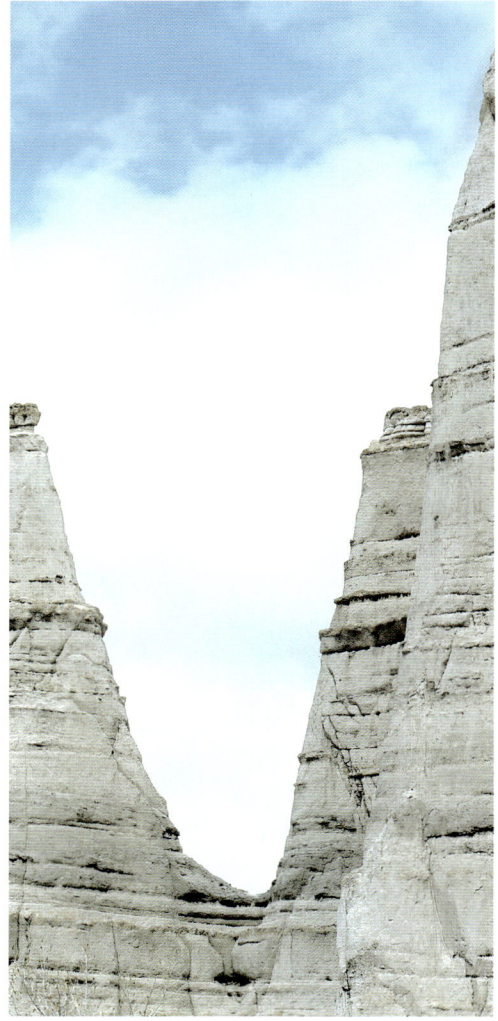

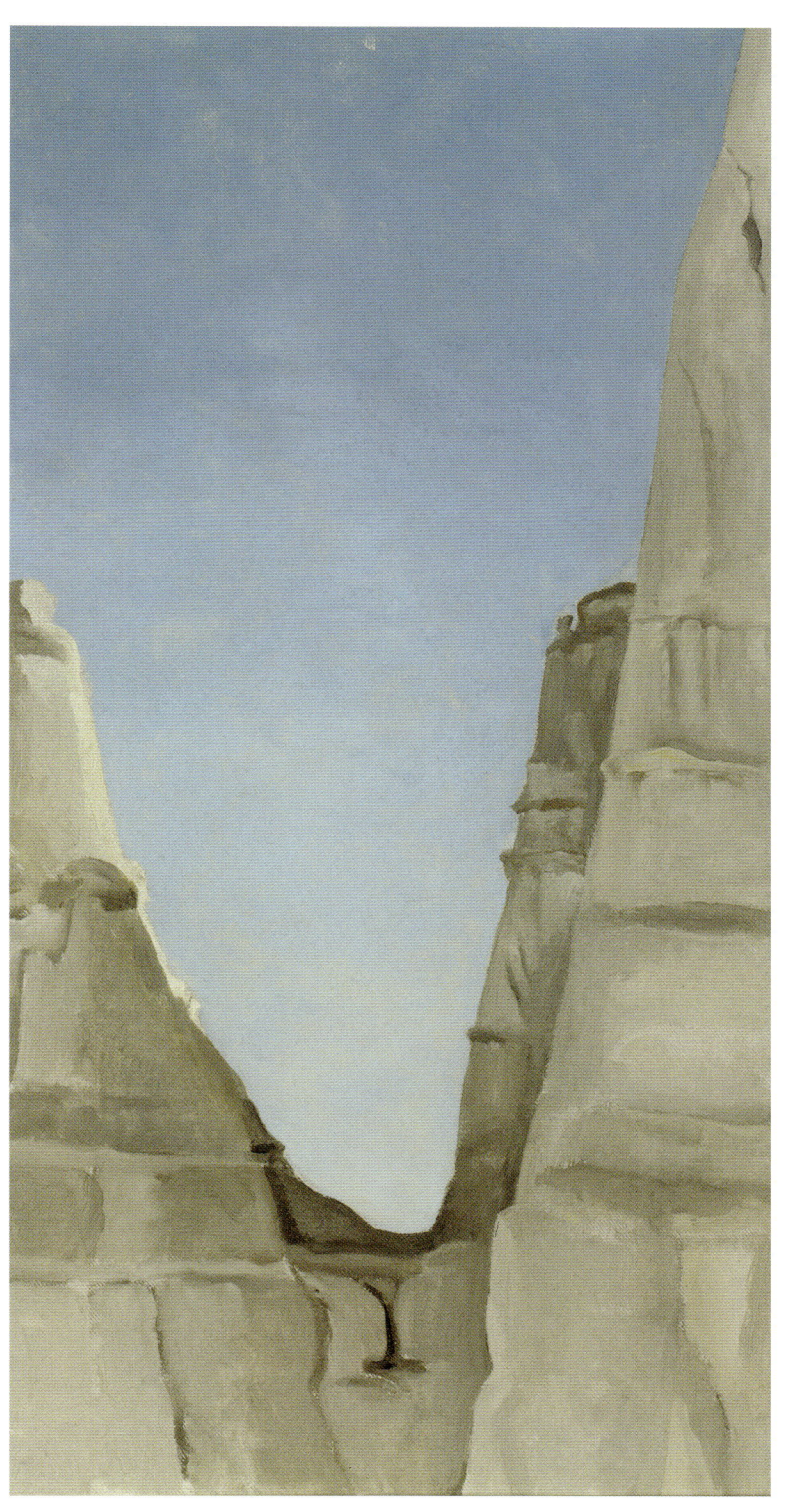

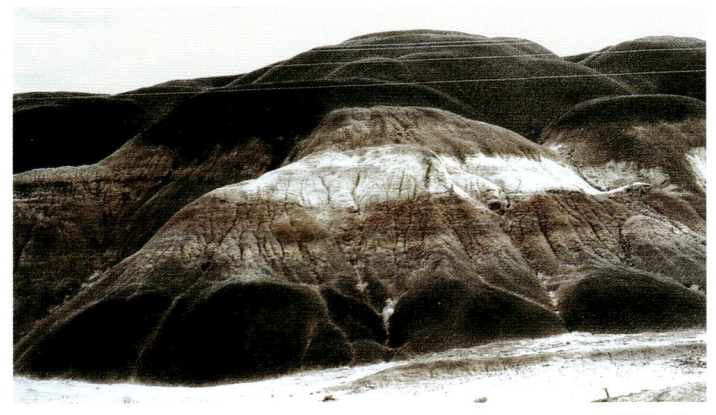

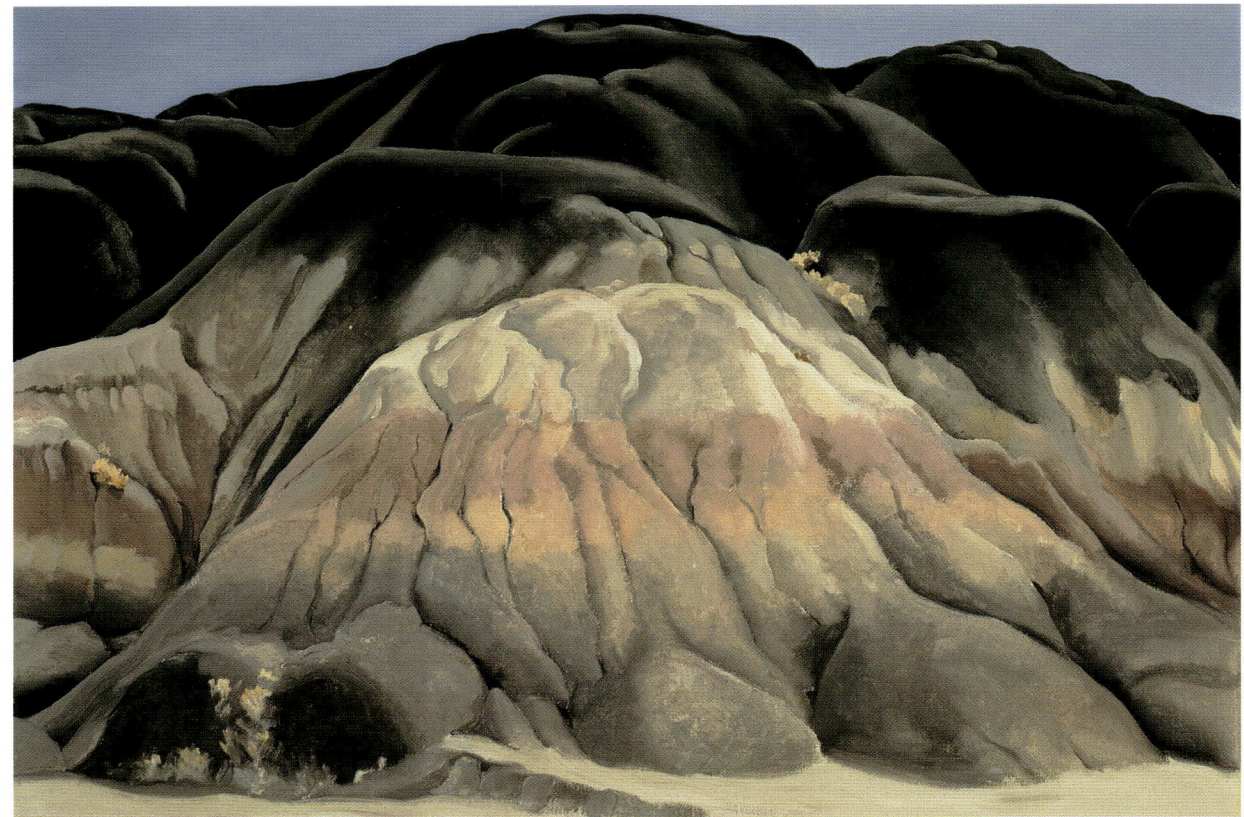

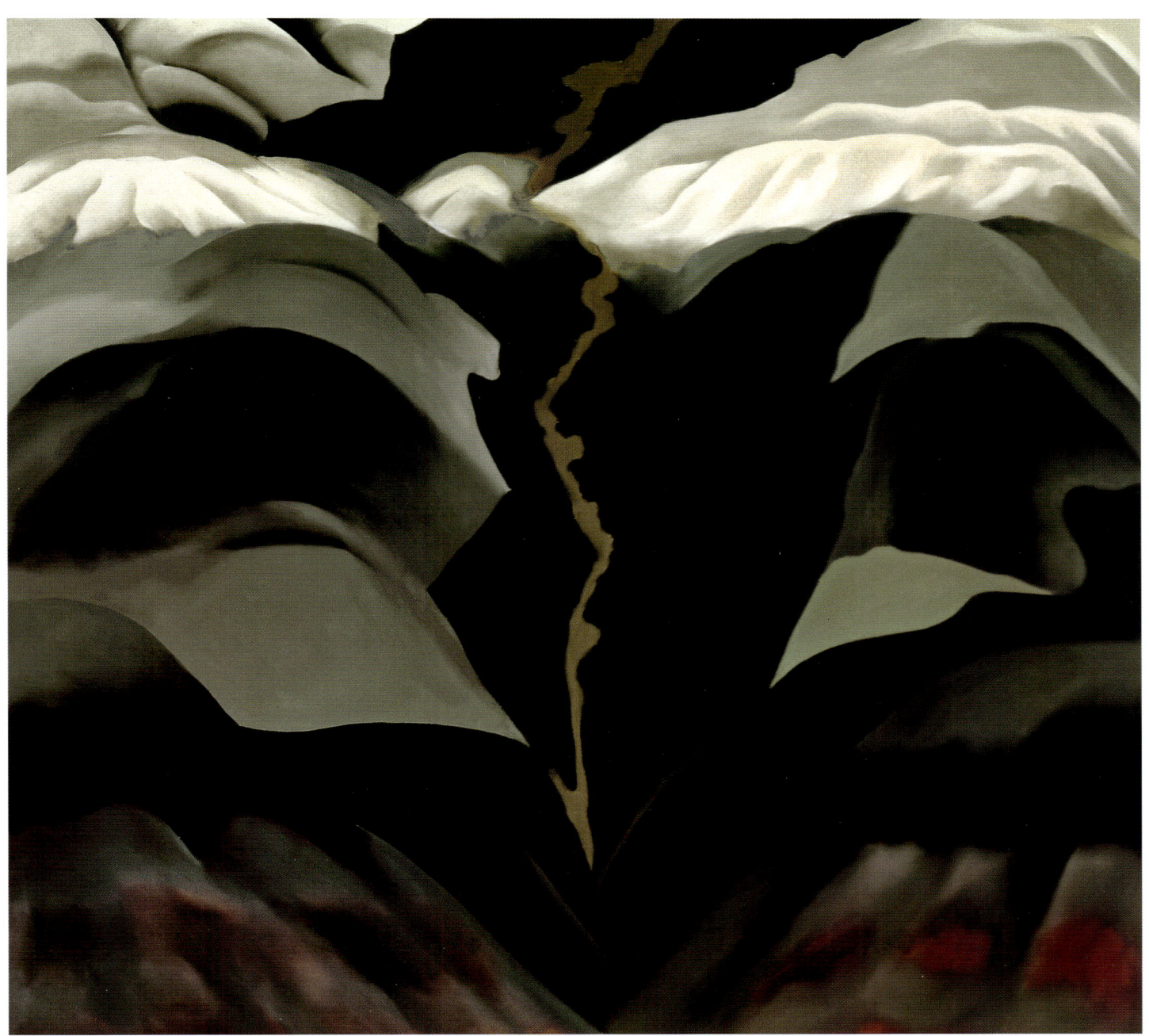

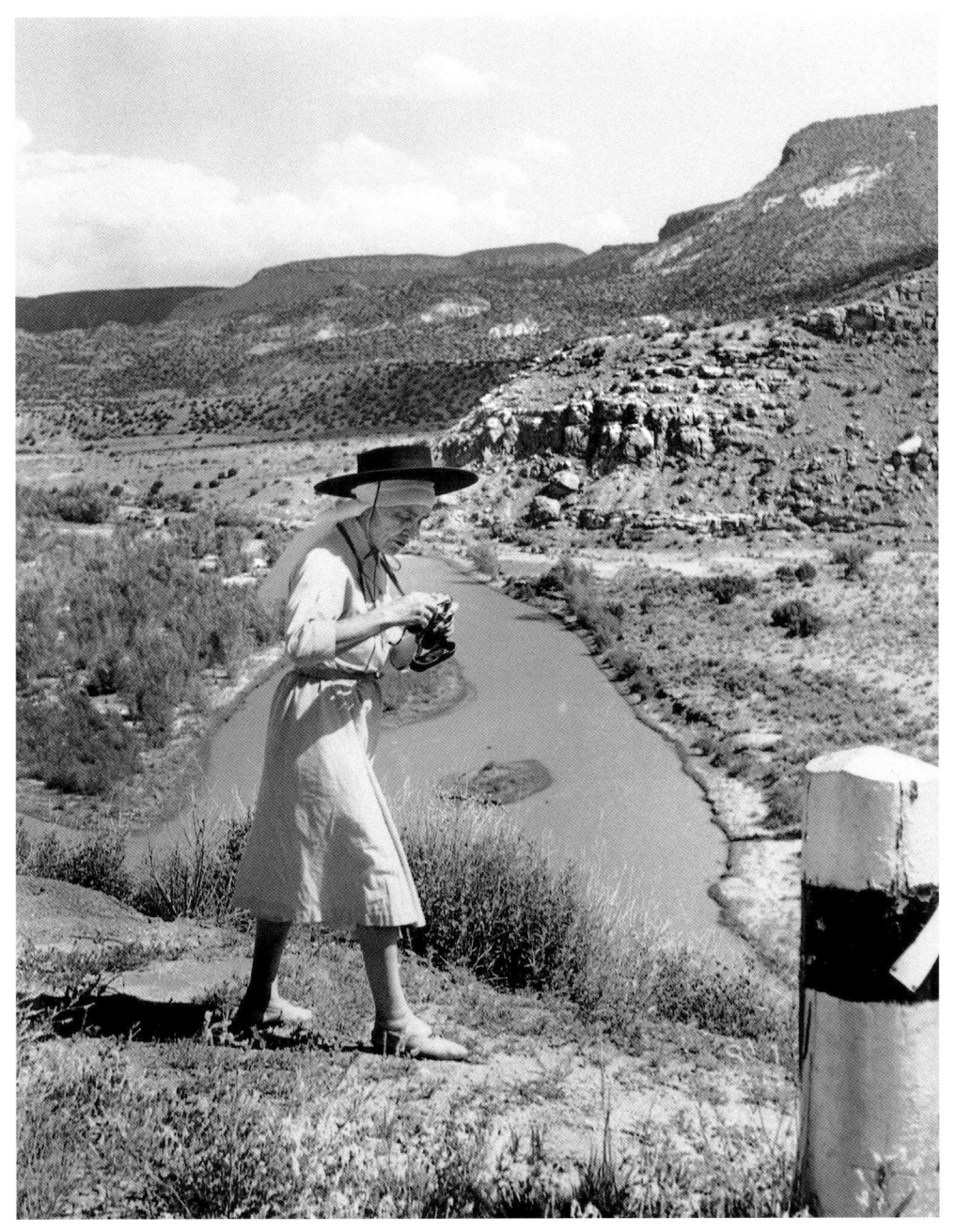

WHAT BECOMES CLEAR from looking at these paintings is that the means O'Keeffe used to achieve them relate as much to photographic devices as they do to painting devices. She cropped forms, compressed space, distorted size-scale relationships, and used tonal manipulation as descriptive controls. Moreover, she often worked serially, as many photographers (including Alfred Stieglitz) had done, presenting the same subject from varying points of view, and in many cases, she isolated forms and depicted them as if seen through a telephoto or magnifying lens.

Yet there is no evidence that O'Keeffe made photographs (or studied photographs made by others) of landscape forms in New Mexico until the 1960s, when her friend the photographer Todd Webb documented her making photographs of the landscape and took photographs of her with her camera (figs. 16 and 17). And in the book she wrote about her art, she pointed out how the photographs she had made in New Mexico in the 1960s inspired and influenced her.[8]

It is clear that O'Keeffe had appreciated photography at least from 1916, when Stieglitz sent her prints he had made of her work on view in the group exhibition he organized that spring at his gallery, known as 291, which had launched her career. As she explained to her friend Anita Pollitzer: "Isn't it funny that I hate my drawings—and am simply crazy about the photographs of them."[9]

O'Keeffe was equally receptive to the work of Paul Strand, which she first saw in 1917 in New York. She later wrote to Pollitzer: "He showed me lots and lots of prints—photographs— And I almost lost my mind over them—Photographs that are as queer in shapes as Picasso drawings."[10] Her offhand association of Strand's photographs and Picasso's drawings reveals her instinctive appreciation of photography as an art form, an idea Stieglitz had long cherished and for which he campaigned assiduously throughout his life.

OPPOSITE, FIG. 16
Todd Webb, *O'Keeffe— Chama River—New Mexico*, 1961

She wrote to Strand after seeing his and Stieglitz's work in New York: "I believe Ive been looking at things and seeing them as I thought you might photograph them—Isn't that funny—making Strand photographs for myself in my head. . . . I think you people have made me see—or should I say feel colors."[11] And later, after studying some photographs Strand sent her as well as reproductions of his work and what he had written about it in two issues of *Camera Work*, she wrote him: "Ive been looking at your *Camera Work*—read your article again—and I like it—think its fine. . . . I love the little snow scene! Why you know I love it all. The prints you sent me—the bowls—the shadows."[12]

Strand had written about the objectivity of photography and how this quality both limited the medium and distinguished it from painting, and he emphasized photography's potential as a source of new and original expression in art. Although it is not possible to be certain how O'Keeffe interpreted what he had written or what she appreciated in his work, her comments about it seem to refer to the remarkable abstract character and tonal relationships that distinguish Strand's work.

After O'Keeffe moved to New York and over the years until Stieglitz's death in 1946, she learned a great deal about photography by living and working with him. One of America's most distinguished and innovative photographers, he was also a friend of other distinguished photographers and had a vast collection of their works. In addition to being able to study these images at Lake George, where she and Stieglitz regularly spent part of each year, she became exposed to the technical side of the medium, often spending time in Stieglitz's darkroom and assisting him. This fact is confirmed in a letter Stieglitz wrote in 1922 to critic Paul Rosenfeld: "Georgia was busy spotting some [of my] prints."[13]

Thus O'Keeffe became aware early on of the total photographic process and understood how various technical manipulations could bring great variations to the final product in terms of framing a subject, delineating contours and defining shapes, compressing or emphasizing spatial recession, and achieving tonal control. She later referred to aspects of what she had learned in the

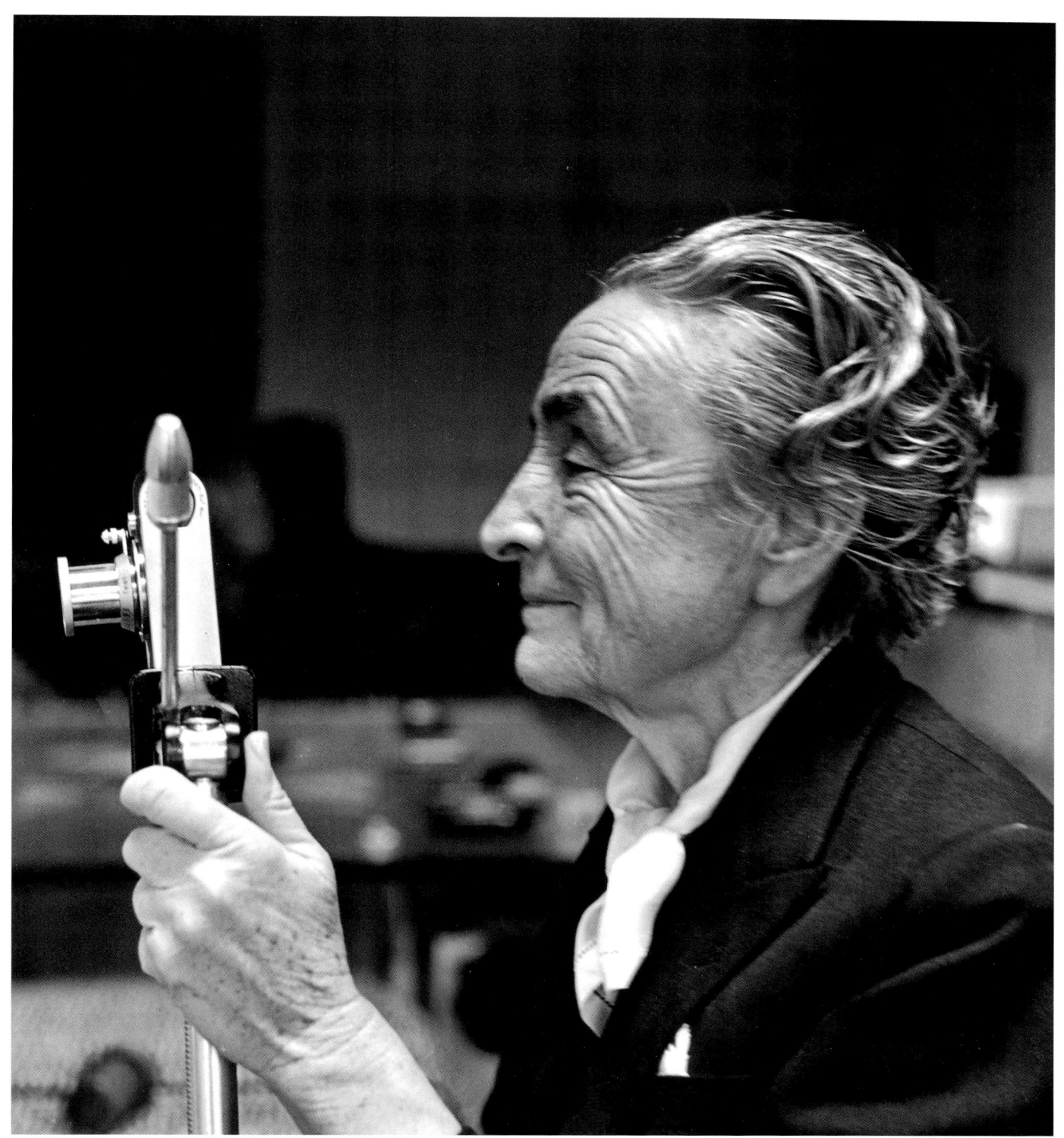

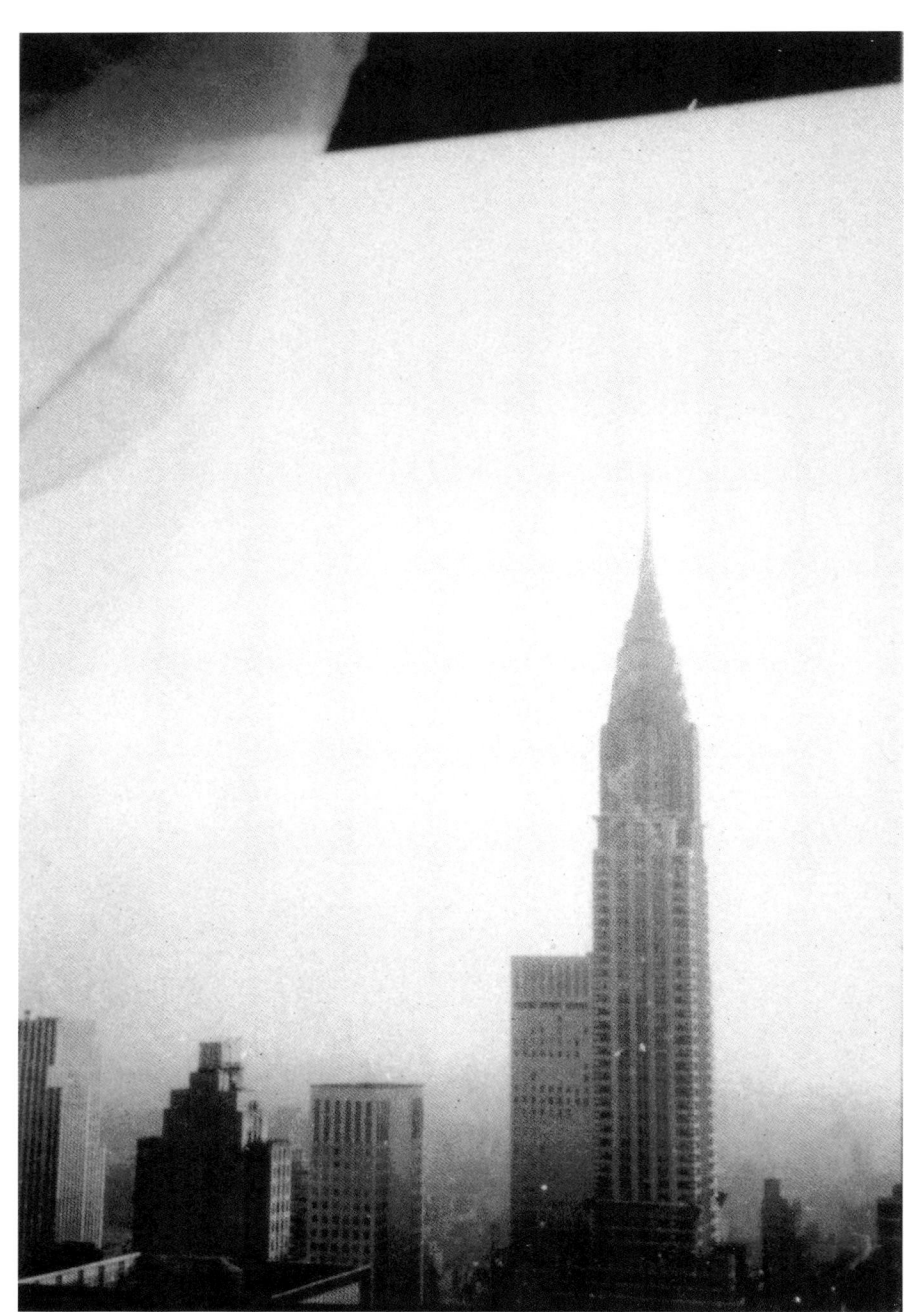

darkroom: "Each print, even when printed from the same negative, could say something different when Stieglitz printed it and mounted it. As he developed negatives and prints I began to learn about a print—to choose the best prints from among the others."[14]

When she was asked in 1960 if photography had influenced her large-scale paintings of magnified views of flowers, O'Keeffe changed the subject. But as Sarah Whitaker Peters has made clear, much of what O'Keeffe accomplished in her work of the 1920s is specifically related to her awareness of photography. This is especially apparent in her depictions of New York buildings and views of the East River, which display her understanding of photo-optics.[15]

No documents indicate that O'Keeffe looked through the lens of Stieglitz's camera, but one can hardly imagine that she did not. Moreover, it is clear that she herself made at least one photograph in the 1920s. Among the many snapshots in her estate is one she almost certainly made of the Chrysler Building from a south window of a room at the Shelton Hotel (fig. 18), where she lived from 1925 to 1934.[16] The photograph relates to her drawing, *Untitled (Chrysler Building)* (1920s; The Georgia O'Keeffe Foundation, Abiquiu, N. Mex.), suggesting that she might have made both images as studies for an unrealized or realized-but-lost painting of the building.[17]

If she made other photographs from the 1920s to the 1960s, she kept this activity a secret, and the resulting prints have been lost or destroyed. Nonetheless, it is clear that O'Keeffe had learned a great deal about photography by the time she started working in New Mexico, and it is equally clear that her knowledge of this medium provided her with a new means of visualizing the world. This may in part account for the clarity and exactness of descriptive contours in her New Mexico landscape paintings of the 1930s and 1940s, as well as for her fascination with manipulating the sizes and tonalities of the forms within them. But the degree to which her knowledge of photographic techniques informed these works, through which O'Keeffe established her own sense of place, can only be a matter of speculation.

OPPOSITE, FIG. 18
Georgia O'Keeffe,
The Chrysler Building Seen from the Shelton Hotel, n.d.
The Georgia O'Keeffe Foundation, Abiquiu, N. Mex.

O'Keeffe was one of the first American artists to explore abstraction as a means of expressing personal ideas and feelings. By the mid-1910s, in defiance of her academic training, she turned to abstraction to develop a visual language she felt to be her own. As she continued to explore the potential of this language in Texas from 1916 to 1918, she produced a series of abstractions that are among the most innovative in all of American art from this period.

In New York, however, her abstractions were primarily interpreted as a manifestation of her sexual nature. In response to such readings, which she felt severely limited the meaning of her work, O'Keeffe infused it with a new sense of the objective, derived in part from her increasing awareness of photography and photographic techniques. And although she was known as a painter of recognizable forms by the time she began using the New Mexico landscape as a stimulus for her work, it is clear that her sensibility was grounded in the abstract principles she had begun developing over a decade earlier. Using these principles within paintings that have been frequently seen as exact depictions of the landscape configurations that inspired them, she created in her New Mexico landscapes some of the most subtly inventive works of her career.

Notes

1. For an assessment of O'Keeffe's response to the criticism of her art in the 1920s, see Barbara Buhler Lynes, *O'Keeffe, Stieglitz, and the Critics, 1916–1929* (Ann Arbor: UMI Research Press, 1989; reprint, Chicago: University of Chicago Press, 1991).

2. For an account of changes that occurred in O'Keeffe's work in the 1920s, see Barbara Buhler Lynes, "The Language of Criticism: Its Effect on the Art of Georgia O'Keeffe in the 1920s," in *Georgia O'Keeffe: From the Faraway, Nearby*, ed. Ellen Bradbury and Christopher Merrill (Reading, Mass.: Addison-Wesley Press, 1992); reprinted in *Women's Art Magazine*, no. 51 (Mar.–Apr. 1993): 4–9, and in Barbara Buhler Lynes, *Georgia O'Keeffe* (New York: Rizzoli International Publications, Inc., 1993).

3. My thanks to photographers Herbert Lotz, Mark Kane, and especially Malcolm Varon for sharing their insights regarding the role of photographs in O'Keeffe's work.

4. See, notably, Jane Downer Collins, "Georgia O'Keeffe and the New Mexico Landscape" (master's thesis, George Washington University, 1980). Recently, a web site inspired by Collins's thesis was put together by Craig Miller; it pictures many of these paintings and the sites that inspired them. See http://www.mongold.org.

5. Henry McBride, "Sees Mountains Red: Georgia O'Keeffe Accused of Misdemeanor in the Southwest," *New York Sun*, 28 Jan. 1939, 9.

6. Georgia O'Keeffe to Alfred Stieglitz, 2 Sept. 1937, in *Georgia O'Keeffe: Catalogue of the 14th Annual Exhibition of Paintings with Some Recent O'Keeffe Letters*, exh. cat. (New York: An American Place, 1937).

7. Barbara Buhler Lynes, *Georgia O'Keeffe: Catalogue Raisonné* (New Haven, Conn.: Yale University Press; Washington, D.C.: National Gallery of Art; Abiquiu, N. Mex.: The Georgia O'Keeffe Foundation, 1999), entry 344.

8. Georgia O'Keeffe, *Georgia O'Keeffe* (New York: Viking Press, 1976; reprint, New York: Penguin Books, 1985), text accompanying pl. 104. For a discussion of the influence of photography on O'Keeffe's work from the 1950s, see Sharyn R. Udall, "Models of Consciousness: Myth and Memory in the Work of Georgia O'Keeffe, Eliot Porter, and Todd Webb," chap. 6 in *Contested Terrain: Myth and Meanings in Southwest Art* (Albuquerque: University of New Mexico Press, 1996), 111–39.

9. Clive Giboire, ed., *Lovingly, Georgia: The Complete Correspondence of Georgia O'Keeffe and Anita Pollitzer,* intro. Benita Eisler (New York: Simon and Schuster, 1990), 174.

10. Giboire, *Lovingly, Georgia*, 256.

11. Georgia O'Keeffe to Paul Strand, 2 June 1917, in Jack Cowart, Juan Hamilton, and Sarah Greenough, *Georgia O'Keeffe: Art and Letters* (Washington, D.C.: National Gallery of Art; New York: New York Graphic Society Books and Little, Brown, 1987), letter 17. O'Keeffe often misspelled words, especially contractions; these have not been corrected here.

12. O'Keeffe to Strand, 23 July 1917, Cowart, Hamilton, and Greenough, *Georgia O'Keeffe*, letter 20.

13. Alfred Stieglitz to Paul Rosenfeld, 22 July 1922, Yale Collection of American Literature, Beinecke Rare Book and Manuscript Library, Yale University, New Haven, Conn.

14. Georgia O'Keeffe, intro. to *Georgia O'Keeffe: A Portrait by Alfred Stieglitz* (New York: Metropolitan Museum of Art, 1978), n.p.

15. Sarah Whitaker Peters, *Becoming O'Keeffe: The Early Years,* rev. ed. (New York: Abbeville Press, 2001).

16. Interestingly, among all of the works Stieglitz made of New York buildings when he was making photographs from the Shelton Hotel, he did not photograph the city to the south until the 1930s.

17. Lynes, *Georgia O'Keeffe: Catalogue Raisonné*, entry 1895.

A SENSE OF PLACE I

TAOS

ALCALDE

TIERRA AZUL

GHOST RANCH

BLACK PLACE

TAOS

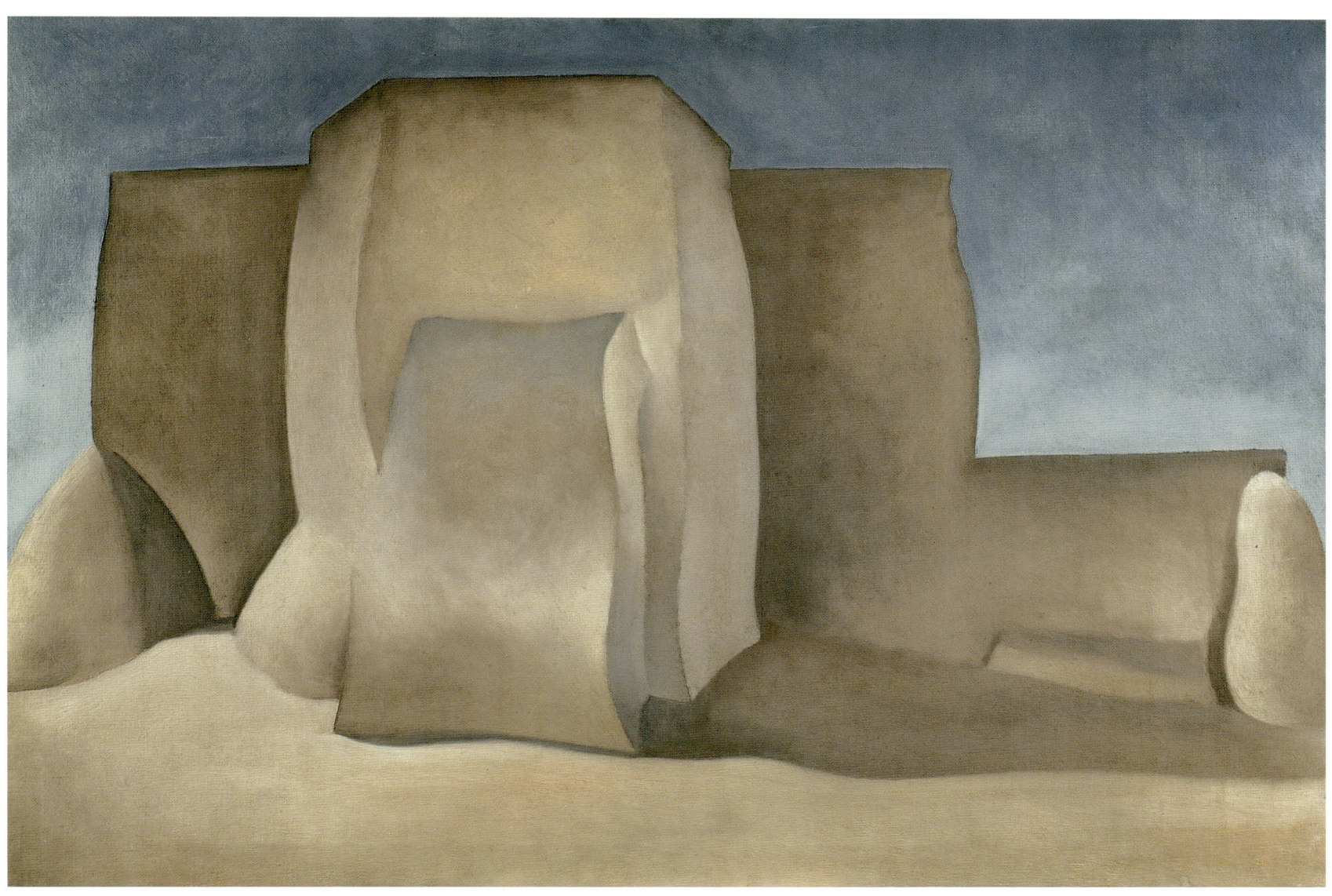

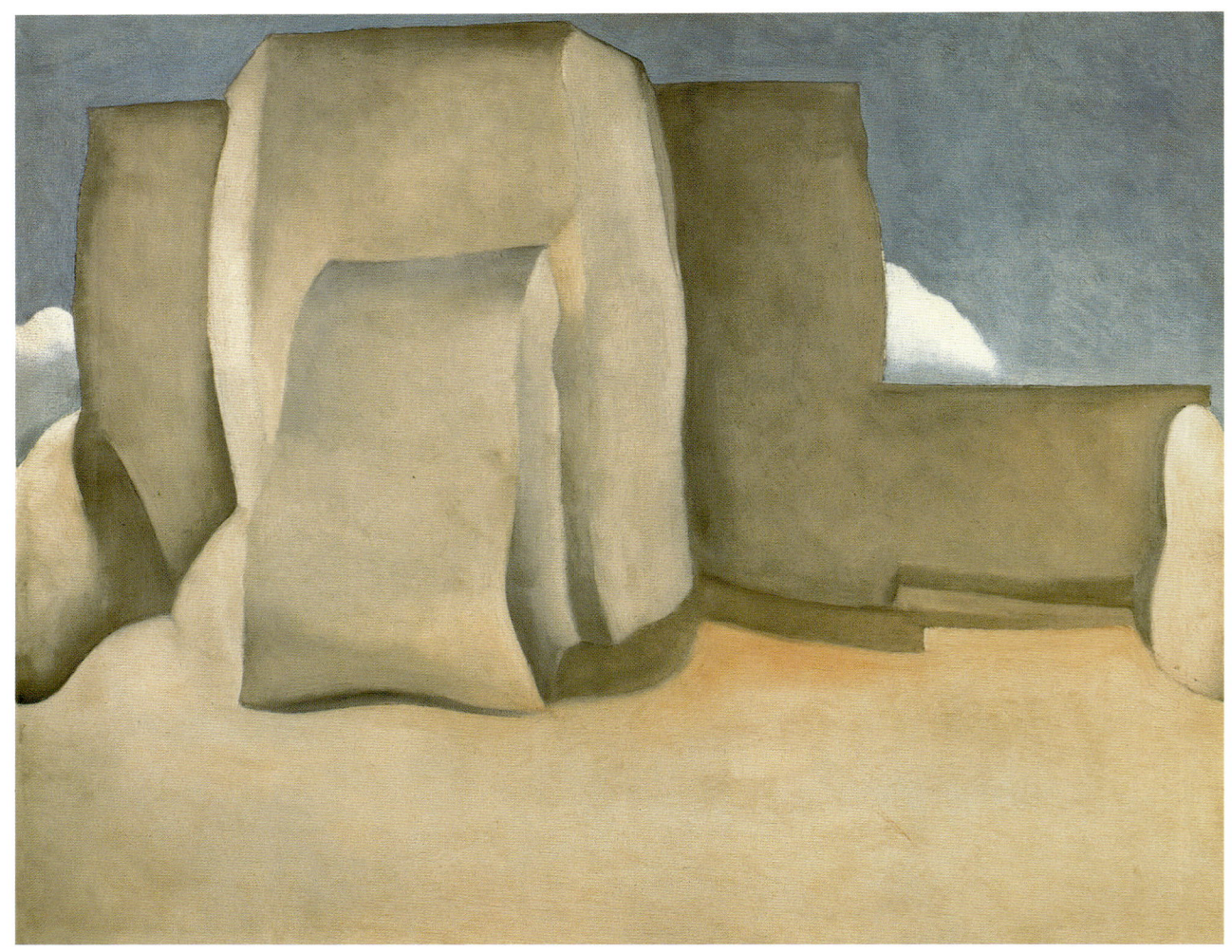

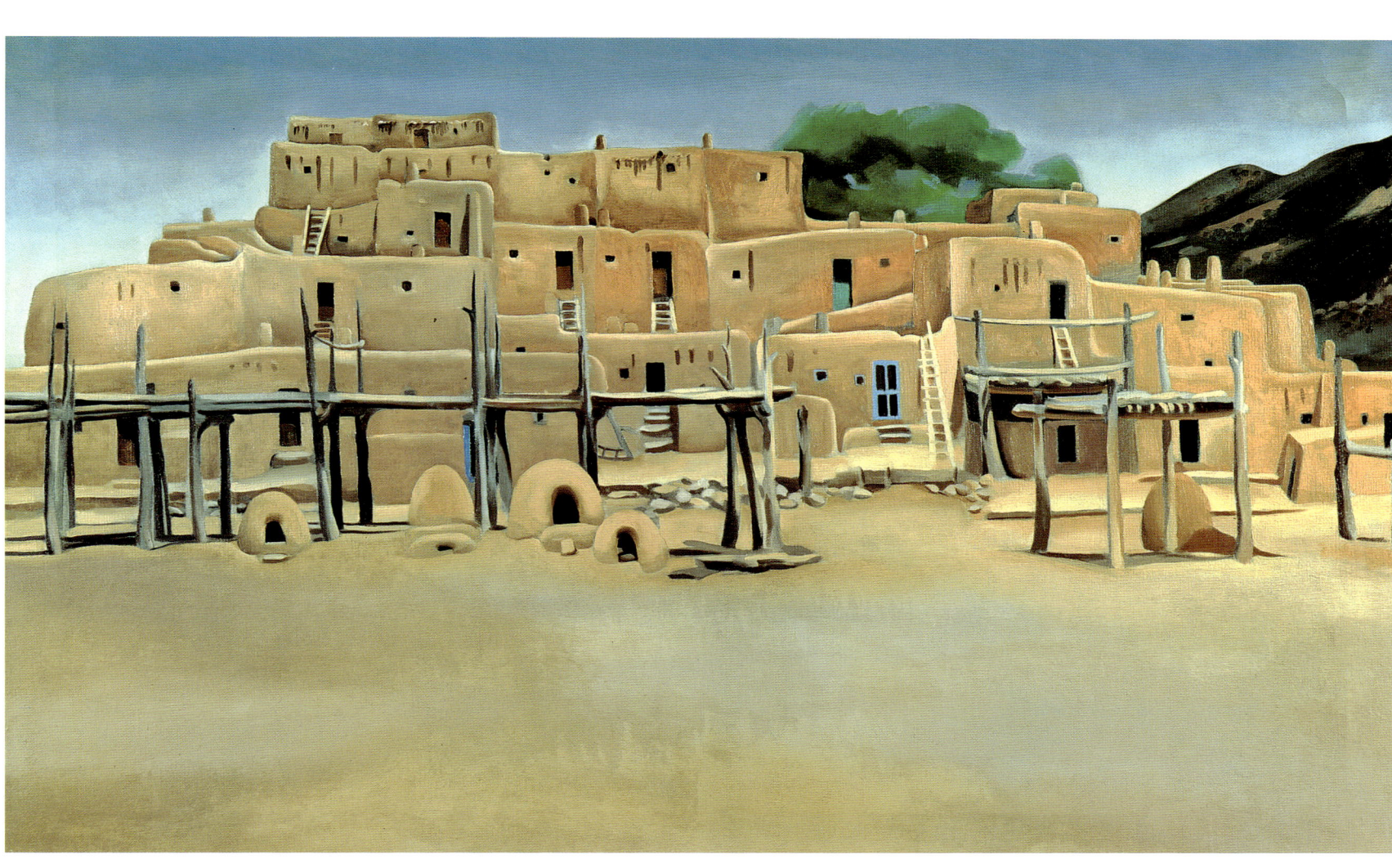

PLATE 21

Hills Before Taos, 1930

Oil on canvas

16 x 30 in. (40.6 x 76.2 cm)

Montgomery Museum of Fine Arts, Ala.

The Blount Collection

CR 741

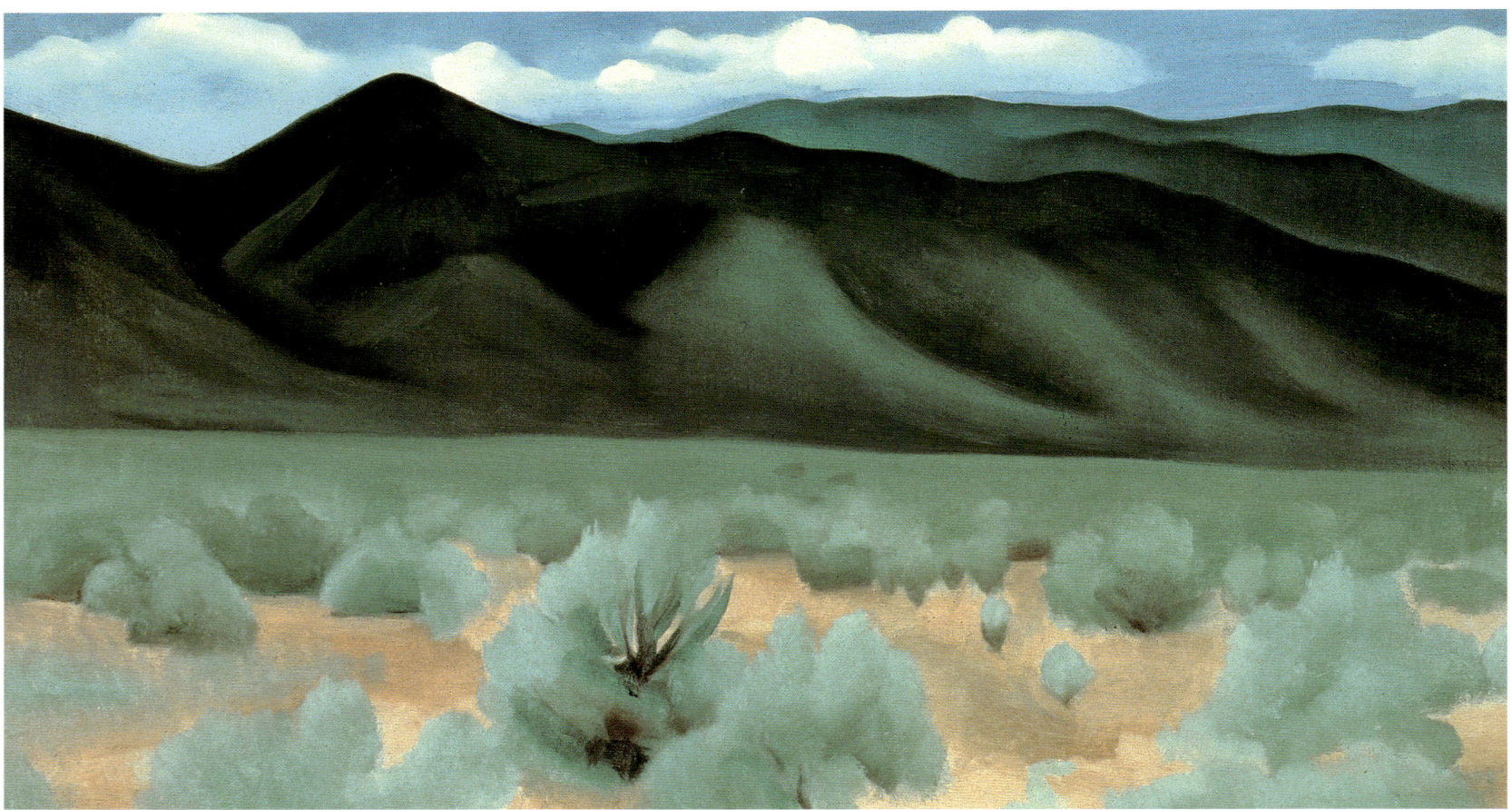

PLATE 22
Taos Mountain, New Mexico, 1930
Oil on canvas
16 x 30 in. (40.6 x 76.2 cm)
Hood Museum of Art, Dartmouth College,
Hanover, N.H. Gift of M. Rosalie Leidinger
and Louise W. Schmidt
CR 742

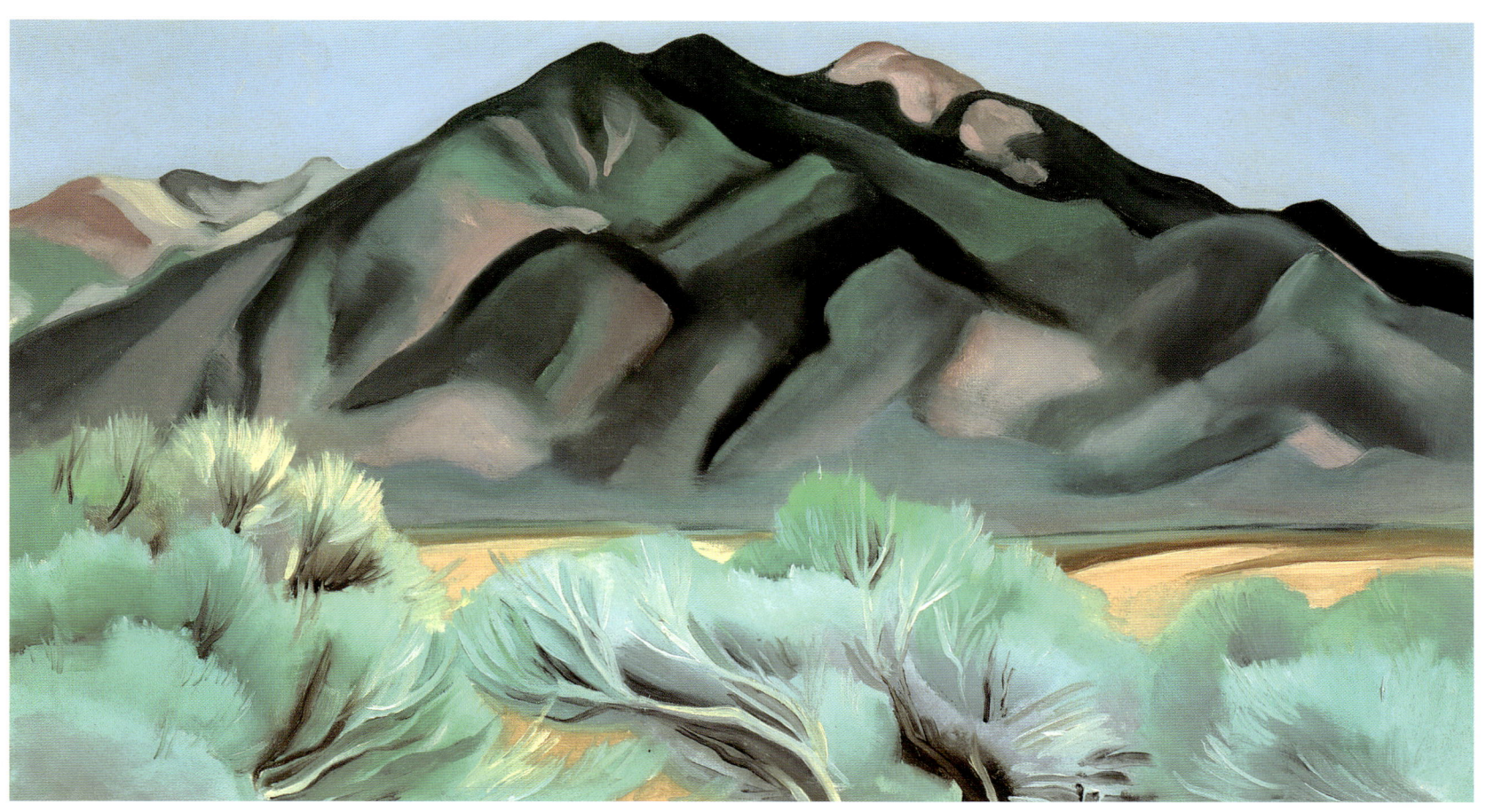

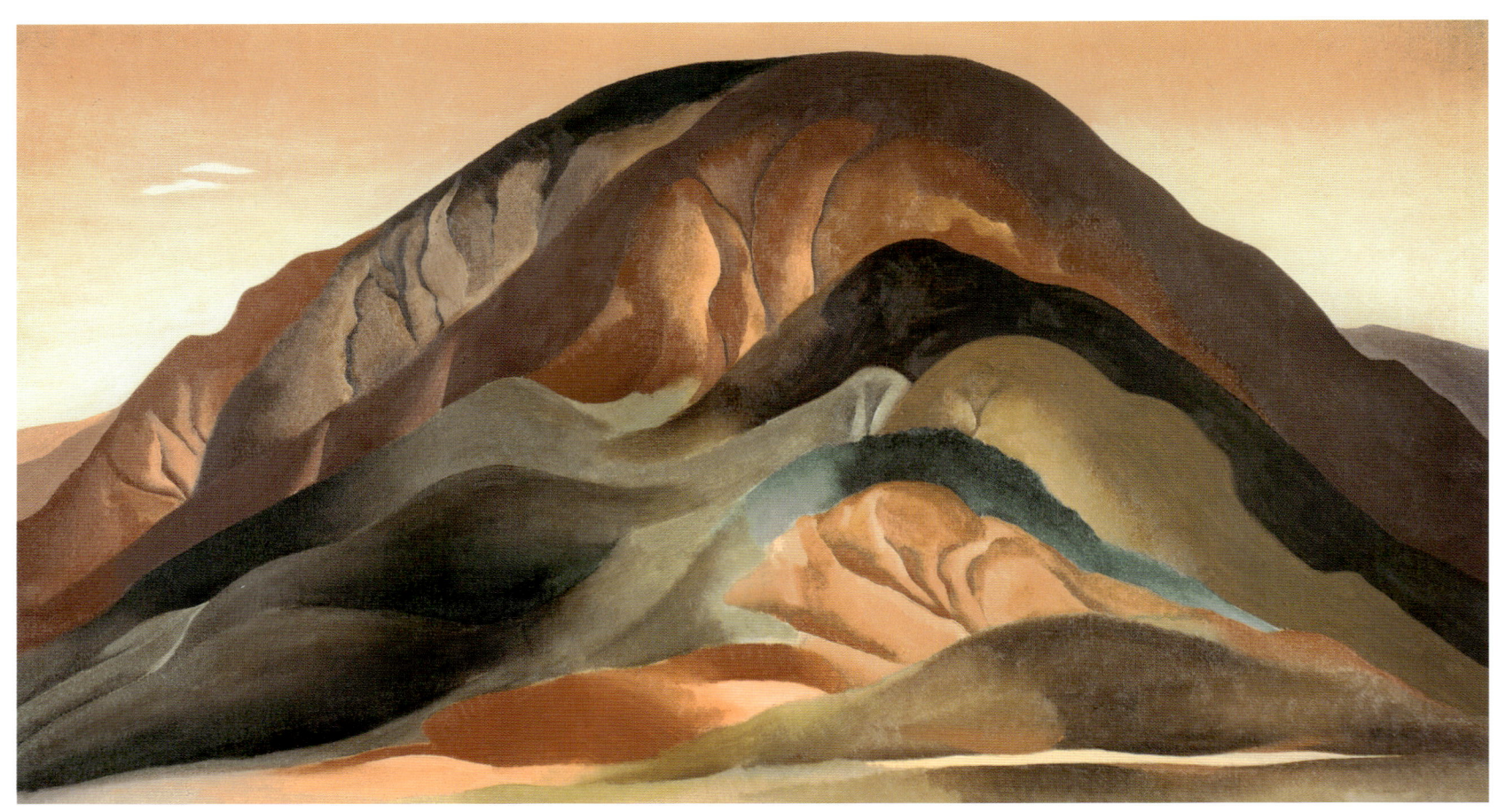

PLATE 23
Rust Red Hills, 1930
Oil on canvas
16 x 30 in. (40.6 x 76.2 cm)
Brauer Museum of Art, Valparaiso University, Ind.
Sloan Fund Purchase, 62.02
CR 740

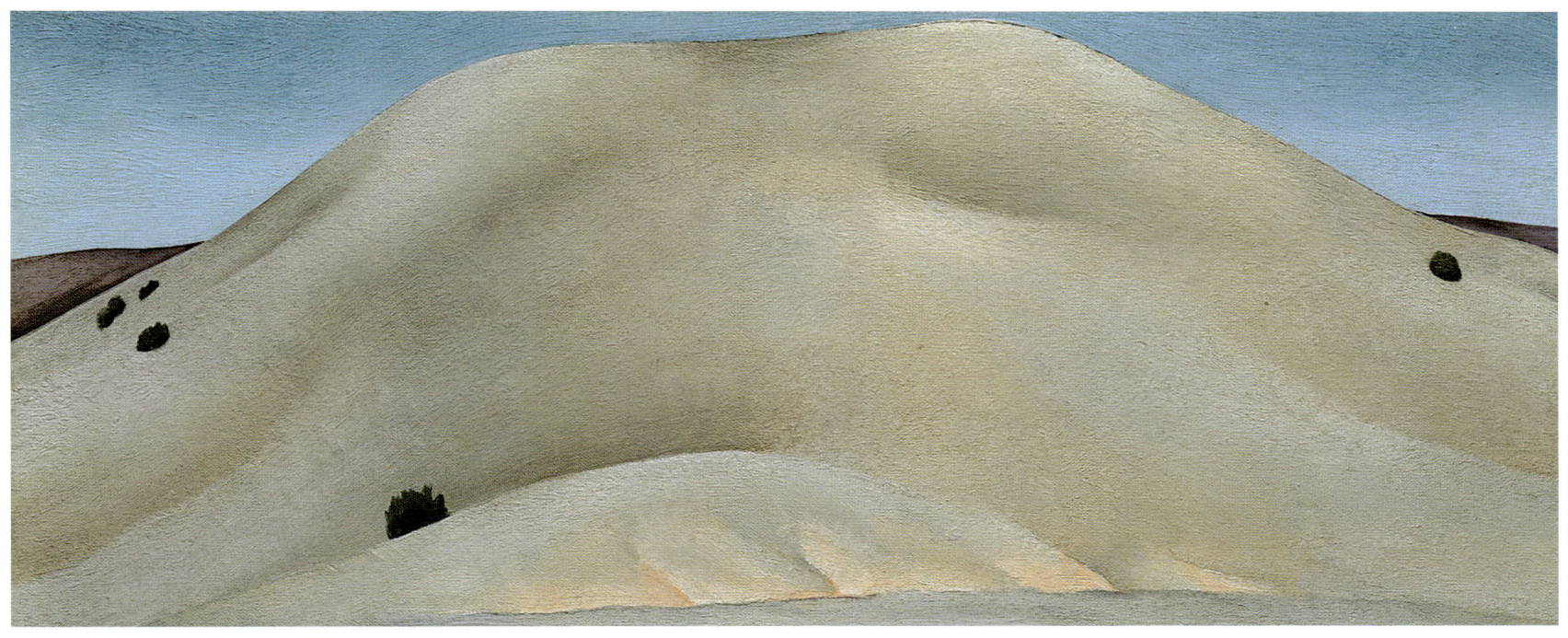

PLATE 24
Soft Grey Alcalde Hill, 1929/1930
Oil on canvas
10 1/8 x 24 1/8 in. (25.7 x 61.3 cm)
Hirshhorn Museum and
Sculpture Garden, Smithsonian
Institution, Washington, D.C.
Gift of Joseph H. Hirshhorn, 1972
CR 691

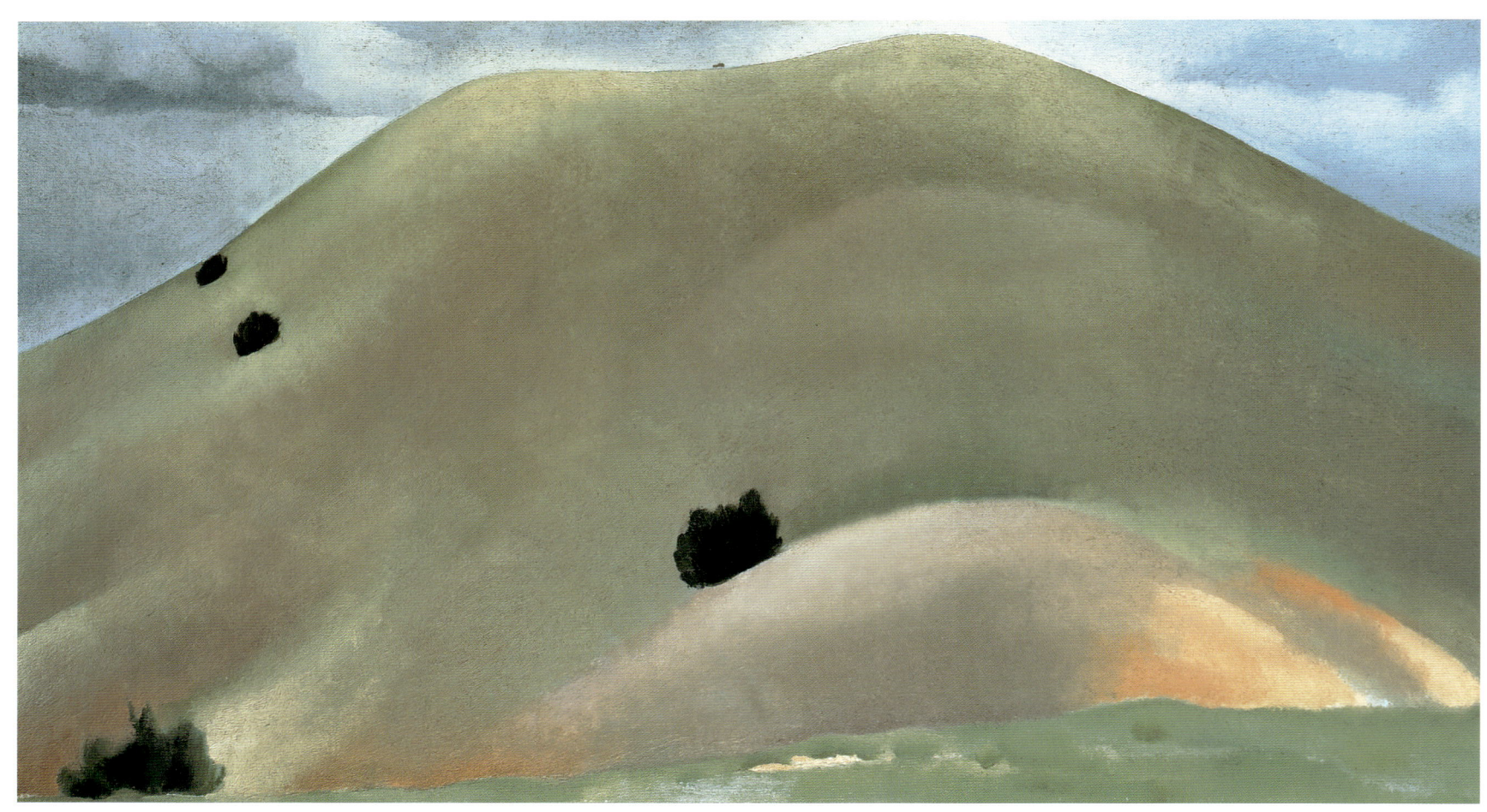

PLATE 25
New Mexico Landscape and
Sand Hills, 1930
Oil on canvas
16 x 30 in. (40.6 x 76.2 cm)
Private collection
CR 725

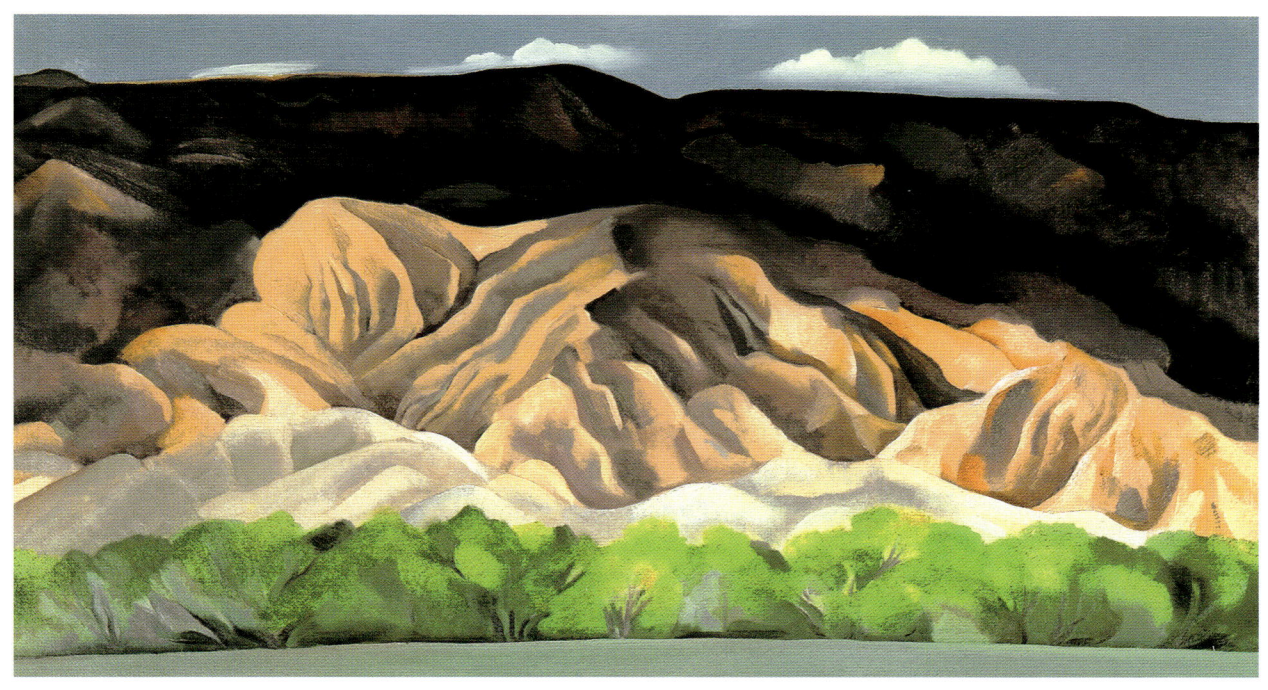

PLATE 26
Back of Marie's No. 4, 1931
Oil on canvas
16 x 30 in. (40.6 x 76.2 cm)
Georgia O'Keeffe Museum,
Santa Fe, N. Mex. Gift of
The Burnett Foundation
CR 793

TIERRA
AZUL

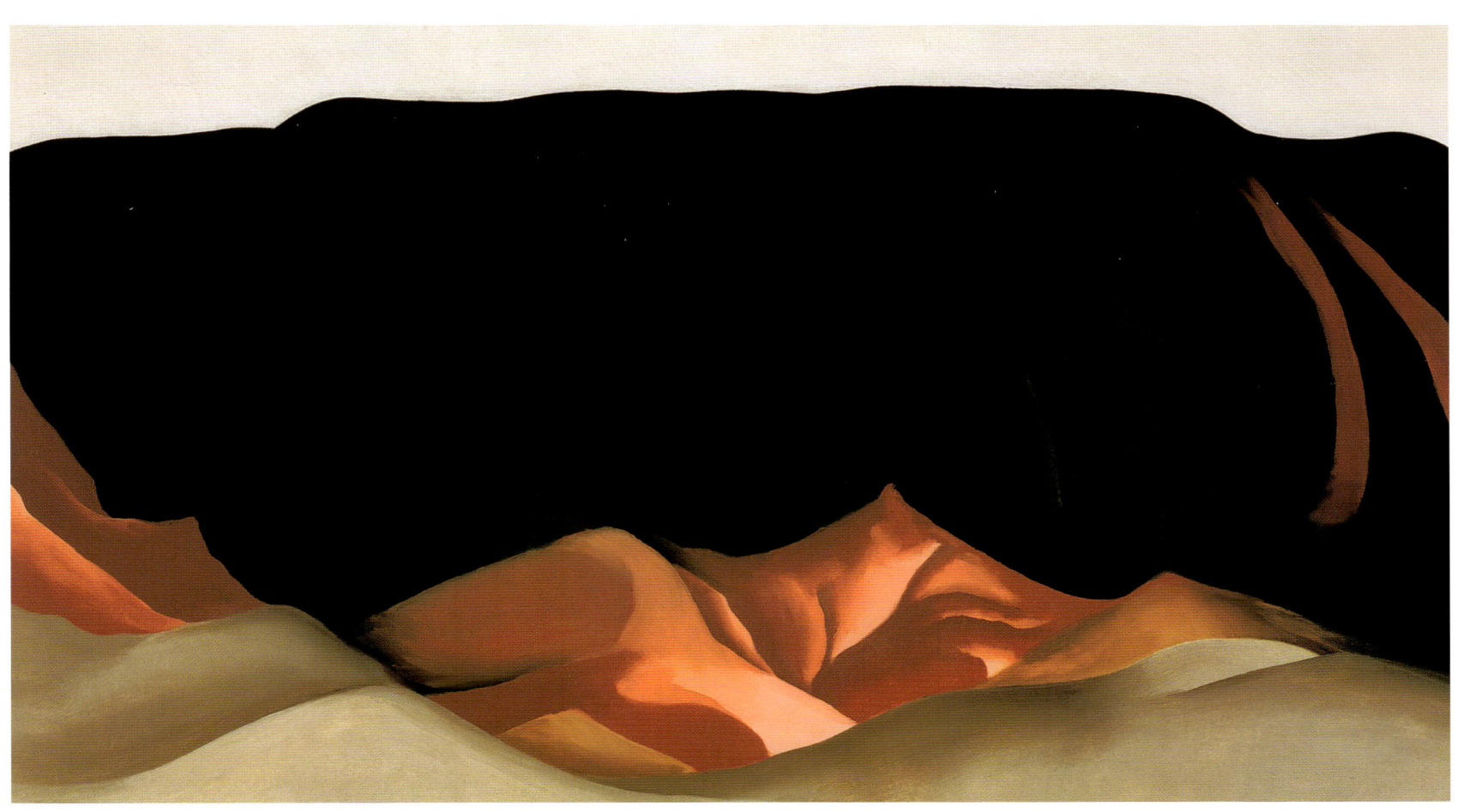

GHOST RANCH

RIGHT, PLATE 28
Purple Hills, 1935
Oil on canvas
16 x 30 in. (40.6 x 76.2 cm)
San Diego Museum of Art.
Gift of Mr. and Mrs.
Norton S. Walbridge
CR 870

OPPOSITE, PLATE 29
Small Purple Hills, 1934
Oil on board
16 x 19 3/4 in. (40.6 x 50.2 cm)
Private collection
CR 838

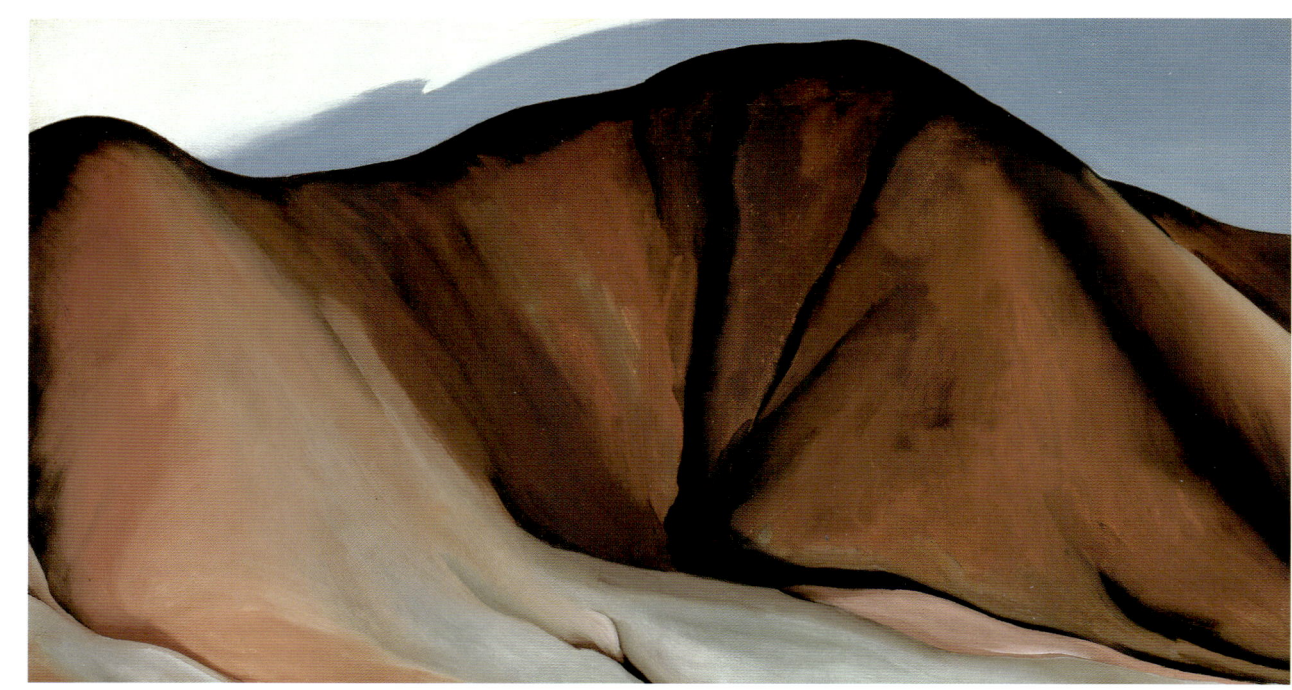

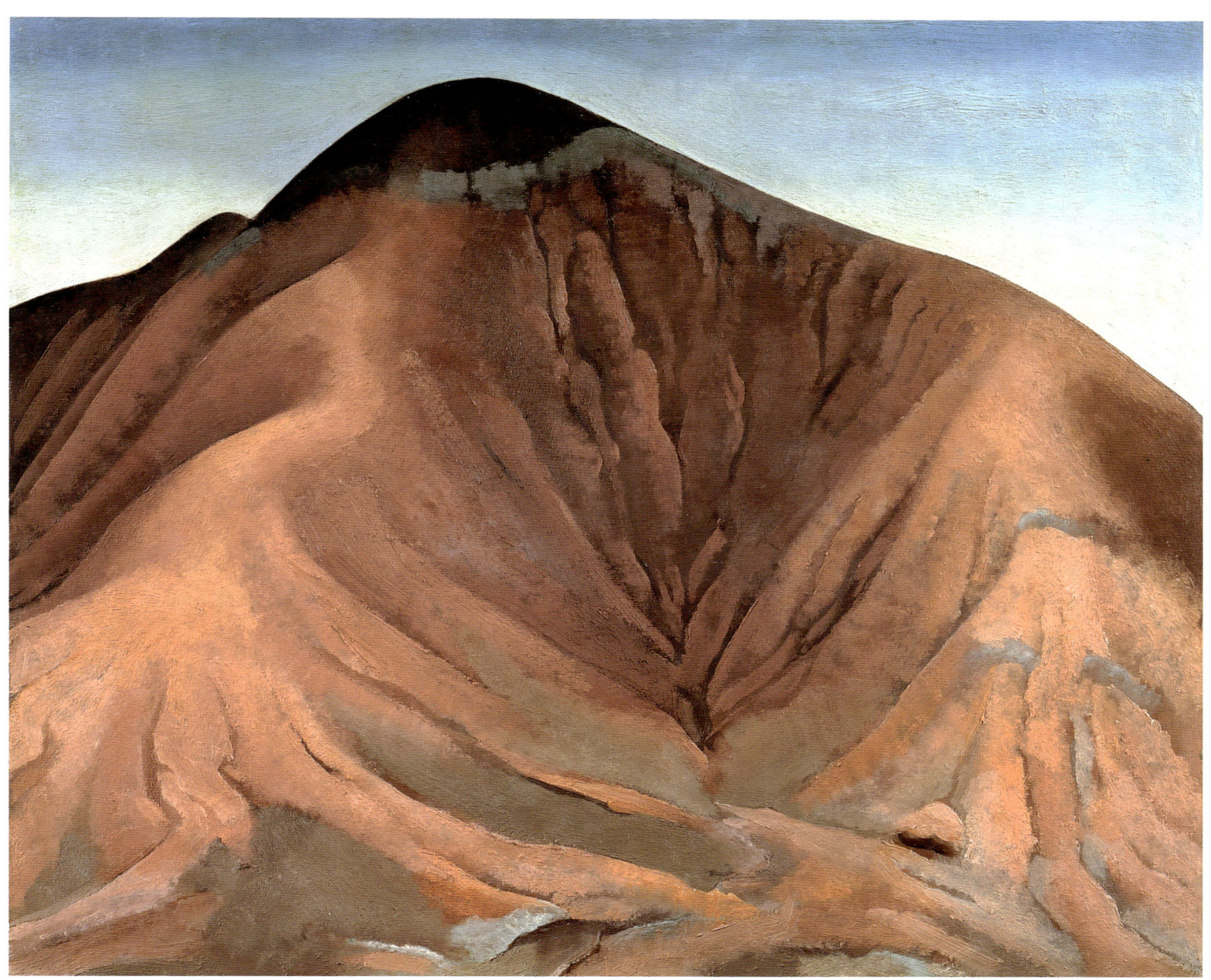

BLACK PLACE

RIGHT, PLATE 30
Grey Hill Forms, 1936
Oil on canvas
20 x 30 in. (50.8 x 76.2 cm)
Museum of Fine Arts, Museum
of New Mexico, Santa Fe. Gift of
the Estate of Georgia O'Keeffe,
1987 (87.449.1). By agreement
between Museum of New
Mexico and The University
of New Mexico, in permanent
possession of University Art
Museum, The University of
New Mexico (P87.1)
CR 895

OPPOSITE, PLATE 31
The Black Place III, 1945
Pastel on paper
27 3/4 x 43 3/4 in. (70.5 x 111.1 cm)
Private collection
CR 1112

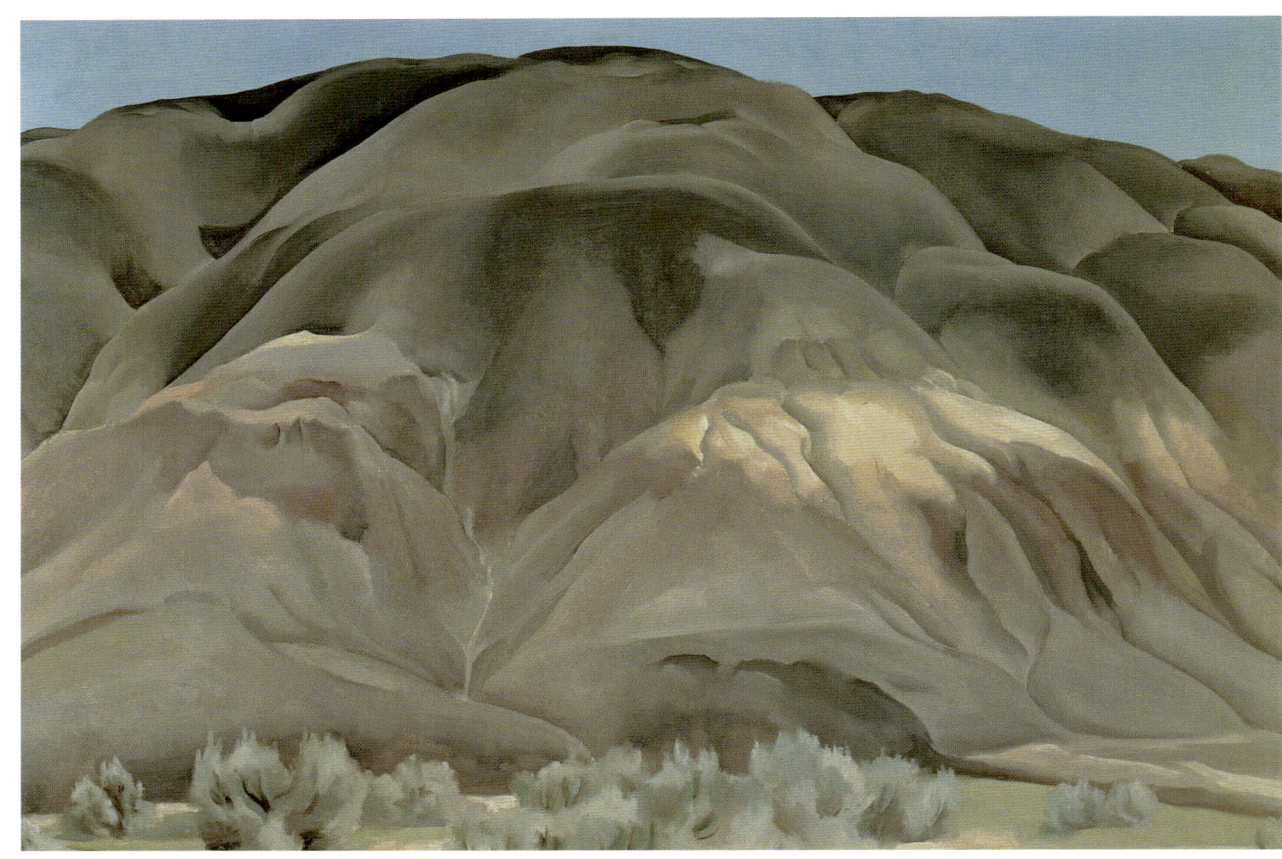

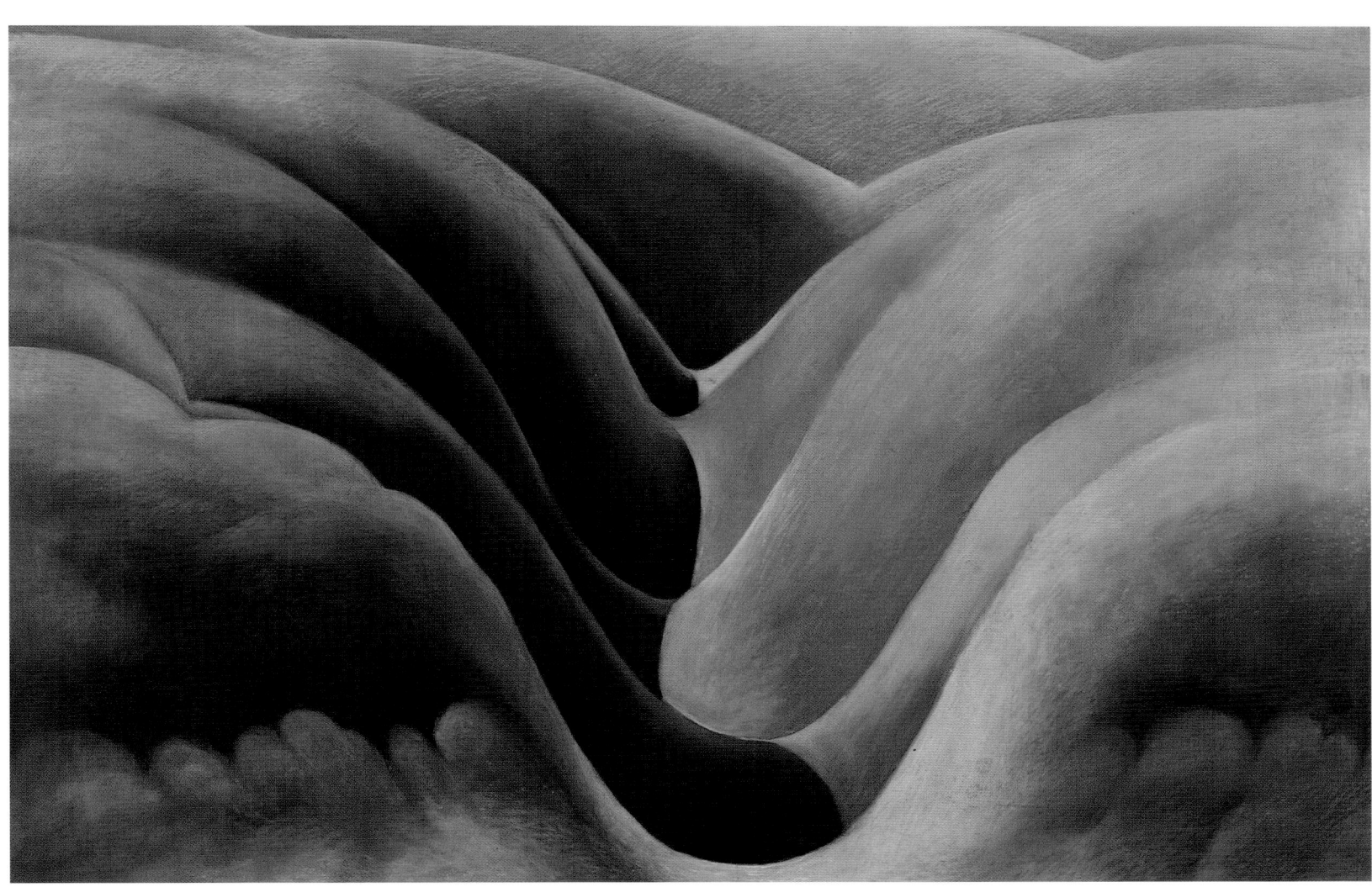

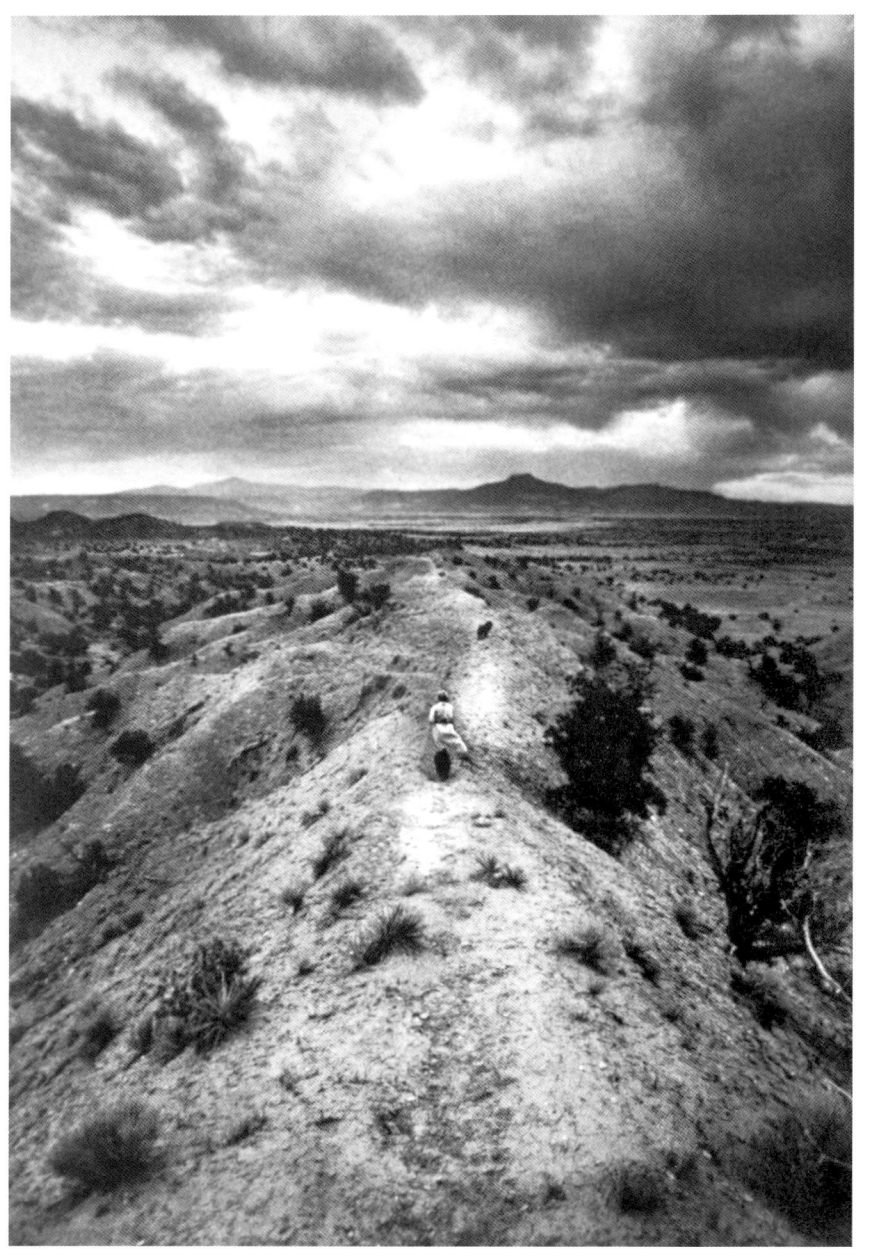

In September of 1951 Georgia O'Keeffe climbed to the top of Cerro Pedernal, a mountain at the northwest edge of the Jemez Mountains, and looked out at the high desert country of the Shining Stone Basin (fig. 19). She was sixty-three years old and had spent nearly every summer since 1929 in northern New Mexico. But she had never seen her world from the top of her mountain.

There are no real trails to Pedernal's 9,868-foot summit, and the ascent of the last twenty feet involves a nearly vertical scramble through loose rock. The top of Pedernal is narrow—hardly ten feet wide at the western end—and the slender *cuchillo* (knife) floats like an island in the blue New Mexican sky. The view of the world from there is spectacular. To the north are the snow-capped tips of the San Juan Mountains, with the Taos Mountains closer to the northeast. Across the Rio Grande Valley to the east are the peaks of the Sangre de Cristo—Blood of Christ—Mountains. To the west, the horizon is defined by the San Pedro Mountains and the Continental Divide. And to the south are the Jemez Mountains, the remains of an enormous composite volcano that collapsed into its own magma chamber a million years ago, as well as Pedernal's sister peaks, Polvadera and Tschicoma. Valle Grande, the caldera formed after the eruption and collapse of the Jemez Volcano, is more than fourteen miles across and is edged by smaller lava domes. Directly below Pedernal to the north, west,

A CALL TO PLACE

LESLEY POLING-KEMPES

OPPOSITE, FIG. 19
John Loengard, *Evening Walk, Ghost Ranch*, 1966

and south are the red and yellow canyon lands of the Piedra Lumbre (Shining Stone), a one-hundred-square-mile high-desert basin cut west to east by the Chama River.

Place—specifically this place in northern New Mexico, anchored by the Pedernal—mattered in the life and art of Georgia O'Keeffe. She had first come to Santa Fe with her sister Claudia in 1917, and although they had stayed only a few days, O'Keeffe was smitten by the country. As she recalled in 1973, when speaking about her experience: "From then on, I was always on my way back."[1]

Northern New Mexico is a land of extremes and contrasts—hot and cold, mountain and desert, wet and dry, dark and light. Visually, the near and far, the small and large, exist side by side. One's sense of scale is reconfigured, even lost. Mile to mile, the landscape changes as quickly and with as little warning as the weather.

The countryside of New Mexico is not a static background for the story of its people. The landscape, and the geophysical forces that have created and continue to re-create it, *is* the story of New Mexico. The topography underfoot offers a continuous journey backward and forward through millions of years of creation and destruction. This region is as dramatic to geologists as it is to artists. The skeleton of the earth is stripped clean of a pastoral hide in much of the country, and the fractures, scars, and bruises of eons of uplift, erosion, and volcanic activity are exposed. This is a primal landscape where "the very floor of the world is cracked open," as Willa Cather put it.[2]

Cather was waxing poetic, but in fact the floor of the world *is* cracked open in New Mexico along a rift valley—the Rio Grande Rift—that may, a few million years from now, help to split North America in two. The elemental forces that shaped this land in the time before time—volcanic expansion and compression, water, wind, gravity, flash floods, sandstorms, and earthquakes—are part of the living story.

Although O'Keeffe knew in 1917 that New Mexico was her country, it took her more than a decade to find her way back. In 1929 she finally returned to Santa Fe and was soon invited to the Los Gallos home of Mabel Dodge Luhan in Taos, where she spent four months. The air of the Taos plateau is sparkling and clear. To the east and north, Pueblo Peak and the mountains of the Taos range reach into the sky more than 12,000 feet above sea level. To the west are lower, rounder mountains—the Cerros de los Taos—remnants of cinder cones and shield volcanoes. The Rio Grande and its dramatic 650-foot-deep gorge cut the plateau north to south. This is a burnt land, a place that carries the marks of a fire-and-brimstone birth. The region's volcanic beginnings are everywhere evident: huge black boulders are strewn across the plateau and down the mesa sides, lying in enormous piles in the Rio Grande Gorge.

O'Keeffe had spent the winter of 1929–30 in New York. By early spring, the vast spaces and open skies of the New Mexico landscape demanded her return to the Southwest. As O'Keeffe expressed it in April 1930: "My period of indecision is over—I a[m] going West . . . it came quietly—naturally. . . . It is what I want to do for my work—and I have been so very well after the summer out there . . . the country seems to call one in a way that one has to answer it."[3]

It was the call of a land of gentle yellow, red, and white sand hills found along the Rio Grande near Alcalde that O'Keeffe answered in 1930. In this fertile valley of apple orchards and chile fields, the volcanic palette that dominates the Taos plateau is replaced by a landscape lightened by pastel-colored sands and clays. The valley lifts into soft hills of grey and pink, and to flat-topped tablelands that fall away for miles toward the mountains. Over several summers, O'Keeffe visited and painted the region of the Chama River Valley near the Indio-Hispanic village of Abiquiu. But it was not until August of 1934 that she discovered the country that was to be *her* country, the Piedra Lumbre Basin beneath Pedernal.

O'Keeffe's paintings of Pedernal made this flint-topped mountain among the most recognized landforms in the world (see frontispiece and plate 41). Although it shares the region's geologic history, Pedernal was never a volcano. Its famous neck was shaped by erosion, while its slender top was protected from this process by a resistant cap of hard volcanic rock. Known as Tsiping—Flint-Topped Mountain—among the Tewa-speaking pueblos of the Rio Grande, Pedernal has held a position of great power in the American Southwest for several thousand years. The hard material found on Pedernal's upper slope has been a valued tool-making material among native hunters since at least 5,000 B.C. Pedernal is sacred to the historic Navajo and Jicarilla people, and it figures in both tribes' creation stories. But previous claims to Pedernal's hallowed ground meant little to O'Keeffe. As she stated simply and frequently: "It's my private mountain. . . . It belongs to me. God told me if I painted it enough, I could have it."[4]

A friend told O'Keeffe in July of 1934 that there was a spectacular landscape at a place called Ghost Ranch, some fifteen miles beyond Abiquiu. With only vague directions as to the exact whereabouts of its guest ranch, they set out soon thereafter to find what O'Keeffe later described as "the best place in the world."[5] Heading west from Alcalde, they drove past Abiquiu and into the deep maroon red canyon of the Chama River. The sudden appearance of these steep rock walls dramatically and absolutely marks the western fault line of the Rio Grande Rift.

A mile farther to the west, the precipitous road steps up five hundred feet onto the rugged Piedra Lumbre Basin and the beginning of the Colorado Plateau. Everything changes: Six thousand five hundred feet above sea level, the pastoral farming country of the Chama and Rio Grande valleys has been replaced by high-desert tablelands of fragrant sage and piñon, and sandy arroyos of cholla and yucca cactus. Red and gold badlands with eroded knobs of sandstone buttes and pinnacles fall into the four directions. And from everywhere the horizon includes some slice of the red, gold, and lavender walls of the Shining Stone cliffs.

The warm colors of this landscape were precisely those that appealed to O'Keeffe. Interestingly, these variously colored layers of rock and stone also illustrate to near perfection the geologic record of the earth's journey through a fathomless stretch of time. From the lowest part of the basin—the channel of the Chama River—to the tops of mountains that rise behind the seven-hundred-foot red, yellow, lavender, grey, purple, and white vertical cliffs, 225 million years of geologic story are clearly told. Descent of the Ghost Ranch cliffs is a passage down and through geologic time (figs. 20 and 21).

"Driving almost daily out from Alcalde toward a place called Abiquiu—painting and painting. I think I never had a better time painting—and never worked more steadily and never loved the country more."

The highest rock is the youngest: The Dakota Formation is hard yellow-brown conglomerate rock and sandstone made from coarse-grained sediments deposited along a beach or coastline that existed here during the Cretaceous period, 90 to 100 million years ago. Beneath the yellow cliffs of the Dakota are the variegated mudstones and interbedded sandstones of the Morrison Formation. These red and pink, green, dusty purple, and blue-grey slopes tell a story of this place during a time of water, and they hold the fossilized remains of the Jurassic dinosaurs who lived in this swampy land 130 million years ago.

FIG. 20
Diagram showing various geologic layers in the cliffs at Ghost Ranch

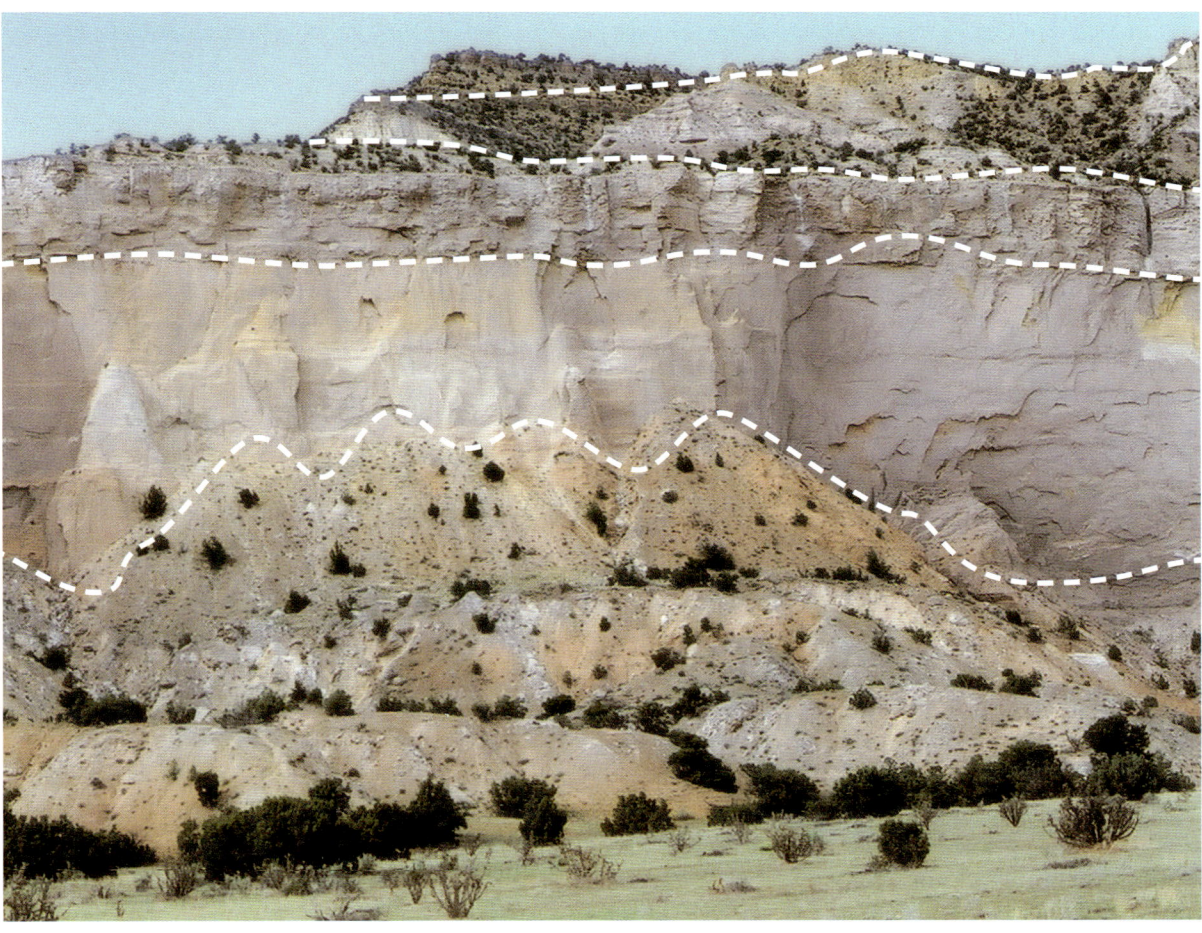

A. DAKOTA—Cretaceous

B. MORRISON—Jurassic

C. TODILTO—Jurassic

D. ENTRADA—Jurassic

E. CHINLE—Triassic

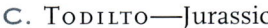

C. Todilto—Jurassic

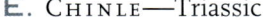

D. Entrada—Jurassic

E. Chinle—Triassic

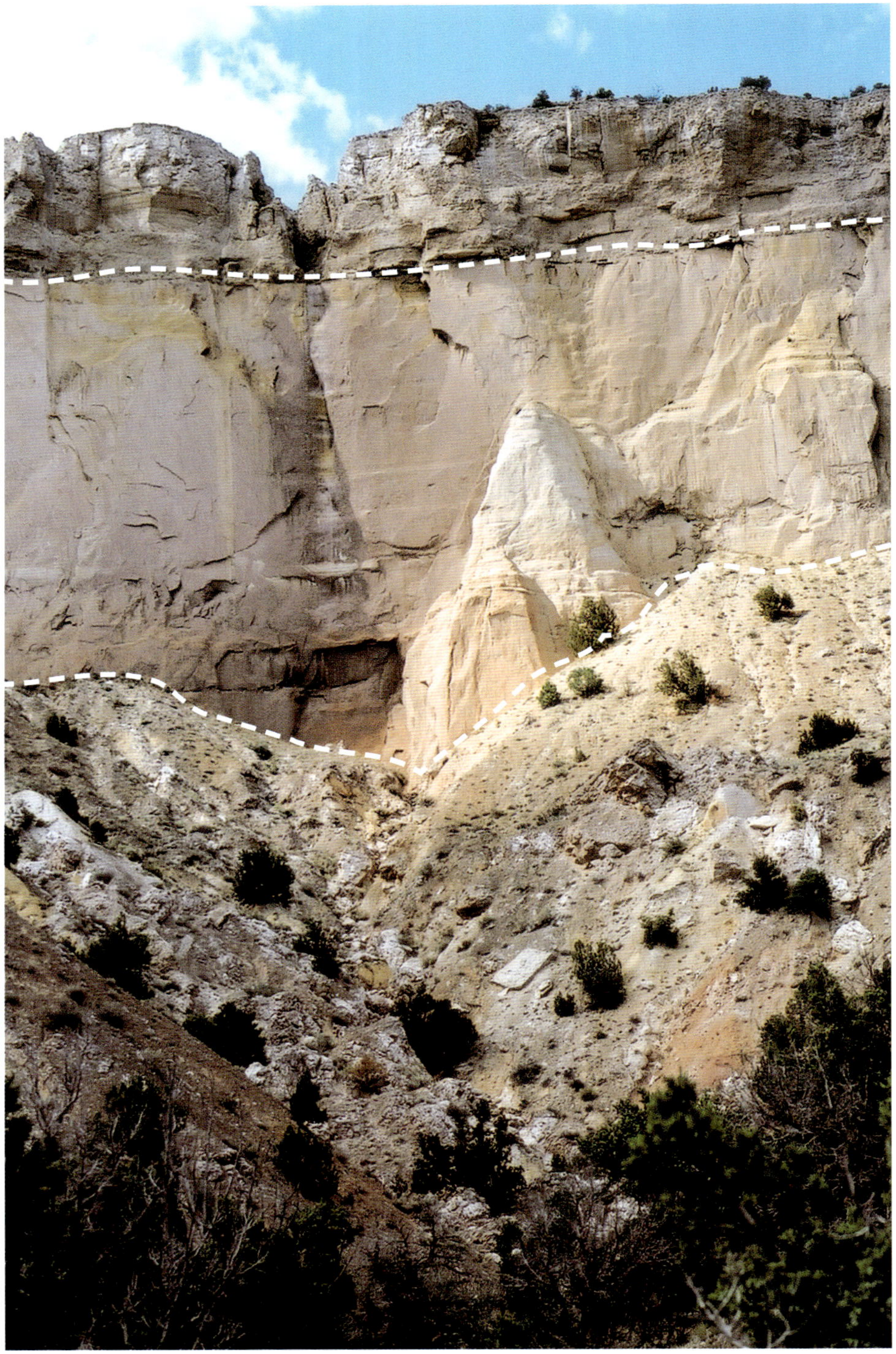

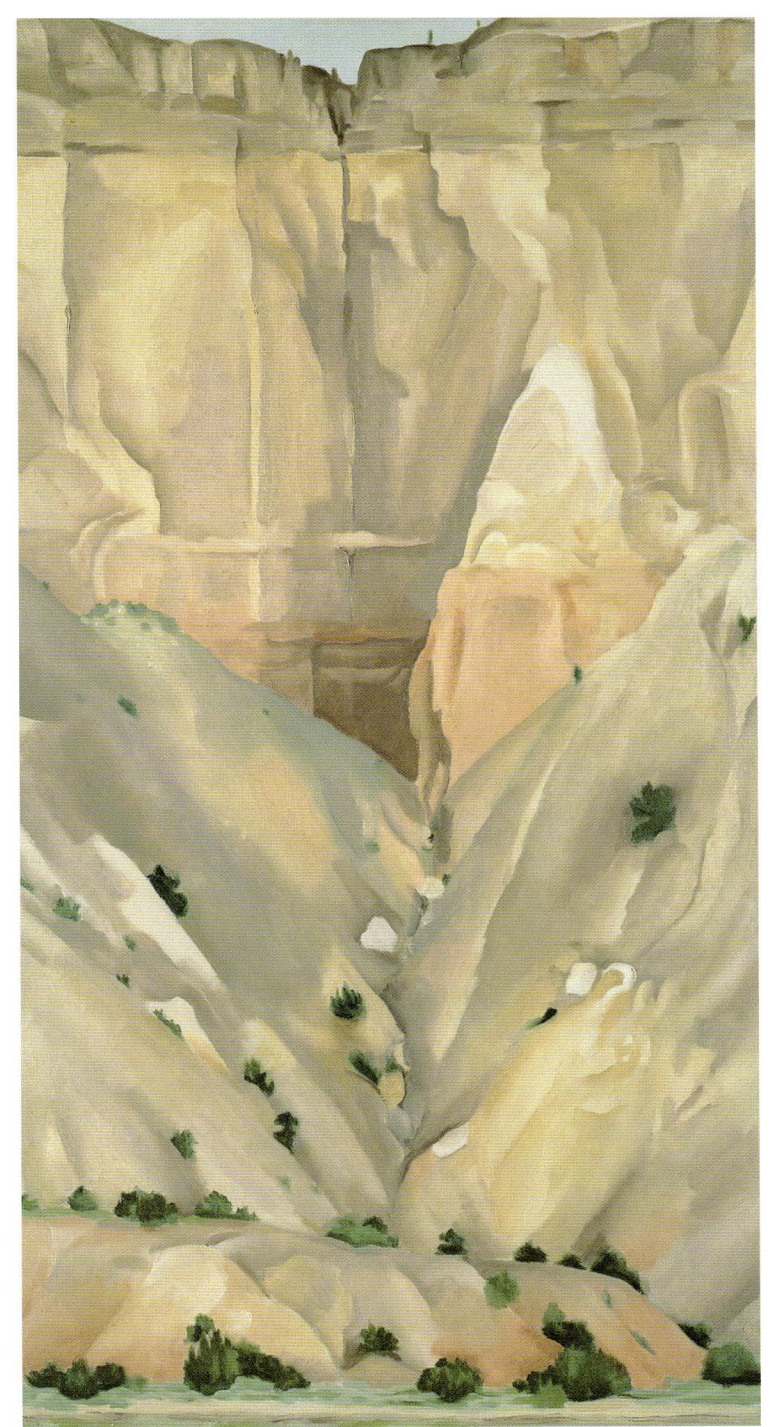

Below the Morrison is the pure white, nearly transparent Todilto *yeso*—gypsum—with dark, thinly bedded limestone. An older layer of the Jurassic period, the gypsum and limestone once lay beneath the lake that covered this basin 165 million years ago. The seven-hundred-foot cliffs of dusty orange, buff, yellow, and white that shine at sundown, giving the region its name—Shining Stone—are sheer, smooth walls of Entrada Sandstone. These cliffs are also of the Jurassic age, remnants of an ancient desert swept and sandblasted by winds some 168 million years ago.

The Ghost Ranch badlands that surrounded O'Keeffe's home and studio and roll away into the horizon are a painted desert of fine-grained red shales, sandstones, and siltstones. Once the floor of a lake, this is the Triassic Chinle Formation, and its undulating red and pink hills hide the remains of life from 200 million years ago. These taluses and nearly bare conical sand hills contain shells, marine fossils, and the fossilized bones of prehistoric crocodile-like reptiles. In the early summer of 1947, the Chinle Desert of Ghost Ranch revealed its most valuable fossil treasure: dozens of skeletons from *Coelophysis bauri*, the first dinosaur.

The world O'Keeffe discovered under the great cliffs at Ghost Ranch would become the foundation of her personal and creative life from 1934 until her death in 1986. Rancho de los Burros (Ranch of the Burros)—a private residence directly beneath the walls of Shining Stone, which had been built by Arthur Pack, owner of the Ghost Ranch—became O'Keeffe's favorite summer home beginning in 1936 (plate 33). The traditional U-shaped adobe house had an unobstructed view of Pedernal, and the red and yellow desert fell away from it in every direction.

On a guided automobile expedition into Navajo land in 1940, O'Keeffe rediscovered an area she had first seen in the mid-1930s, a barren area she came to call the Black Place. This country is not part of the Piedra Lumbre Basin but lies 150 miles to the west—a hard day's drive in the 1940s—up and over the Continental Divide. The undulating barren grey-black hills of the Black Place, which were also formed by volcanic eruptions, form a world unto itself—black and grey hills with, as O'Keeffe pointed out in 1976, "almost white sand at their feet."[6] Its clay and gypsum forms

"[It is] . . . perfectly mad looking country—hills and cliffs and washes too crazy to imagine all thrown up into the air by God and let tumble where they would. It was certainly as spectacular as anything I've ever seen— and that was pretty good."

OPPOSITE, PLATE 33
Patio No. II, 1940
Oil on canvas
24 x 19 in. (61 x 76.2 cm)
Jean and Alvin Snowiss
Collection
CR 985

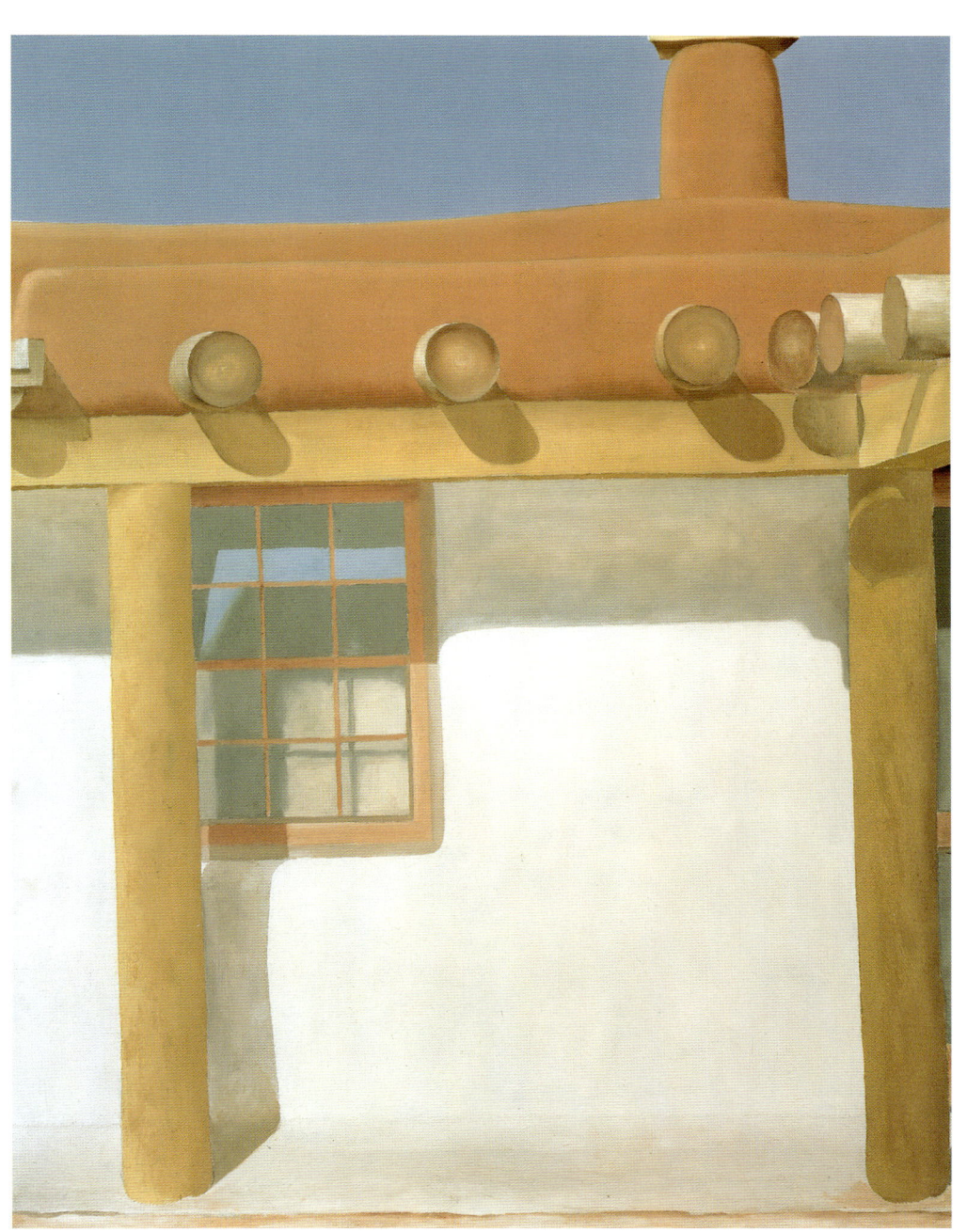

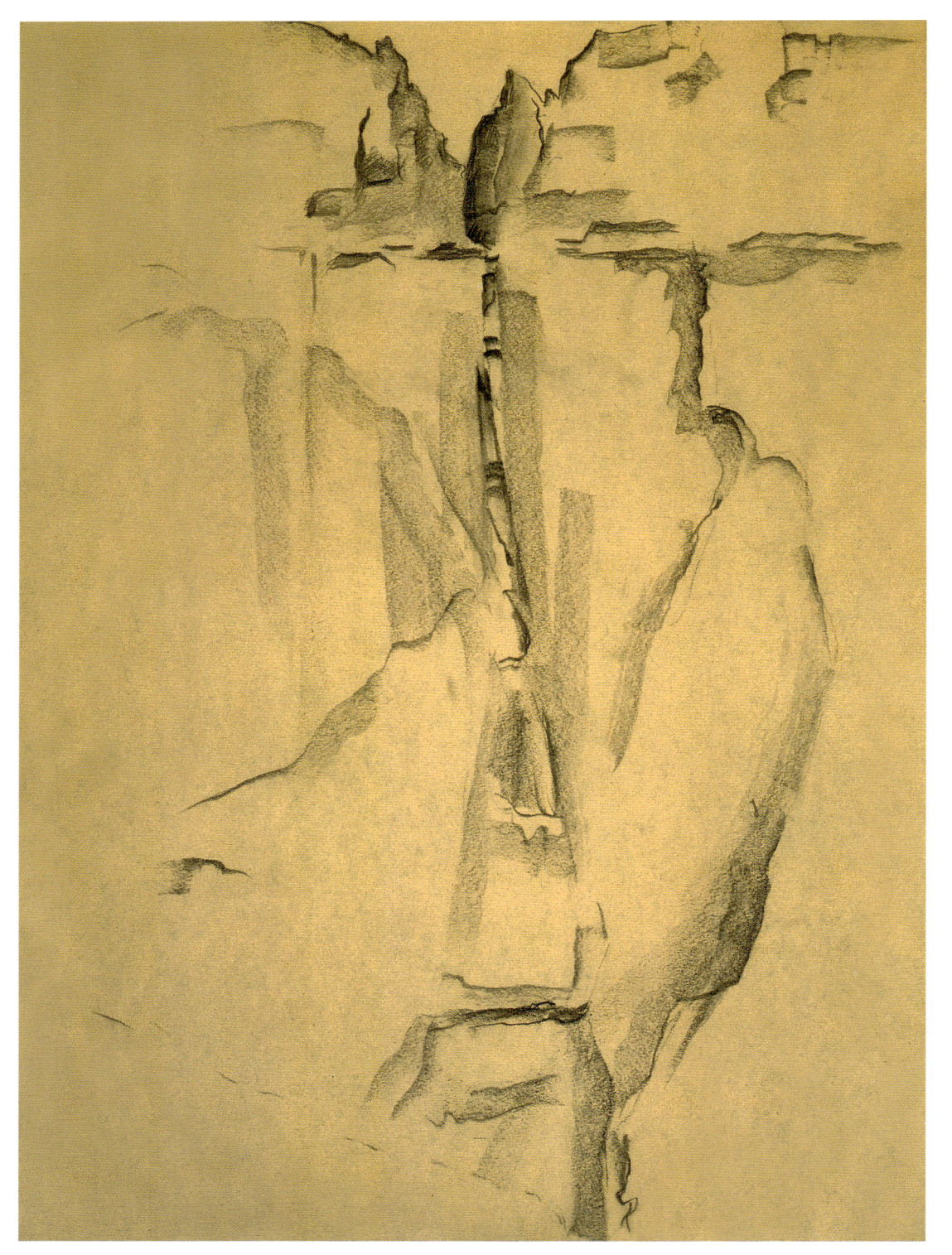

are similar in shape and size. There are no trees, and the hard-packed hills are nearly devoid of even the scruffiest vegetation.

With so little vegetation, it is the angle and intensity of light and shadow that visually demonstrate the changes of the seasons at the Black Place. However, in winter, the cold and wind of the Black Place can be bone-chilling, and in summer the sun and heat are absorbed and multiplied by the black earth, making the place an oven. To O'Keeffe, the difficulties of distance, weather, and remoteness associated with the Black Place were part of its power. A visit to the Black Place demanded a several-day camping excursion from Ghost Ranch, which she often made in the 1940s with her friend Maria Chabot. The nearest community was the trading post at Nageezi, and across the sand land to the south and west was the field camp at Chaco Canyon.

Closer to home was the country of grey-white palisade cliffs and canyons O'Keeffe named the White Place. This wind-, water-, and time-sculpted and eroded region is made of Abiquiu Tuff, rock formed of compacted volcanic ash and cinders in the middle Tertiary period, some 30 million years or so ago. Located across the Chama River from the village of Abiquiu, these labyrinthine formations are as light in tone as the Black Place is dark.

O'Keeffe purchased the Rancho de los Burros house at Ghost Ranch in 1940 and an old adobe house with irrigation rights in the village of Abiquiu in 1945. She especially loved the garden at the Abiquiu house, but the spare adobe in the remote badlands under the cliffs at Ghost Ranch was always her preferred home.

In 1949, several years after her husband's death, O'Keeffe moved everything she owned to New Mexico. She continued to walk into the hot red hills at Ghost Ranch until she was more than ninety years of age. In 1967 she commented: "When I think of death I only regret that I will not be able to see this beautiful country anymore, unless the Indians are right and my spirit will walk here after I'm gone."[7]

"Those hills! They go on and on—it was like looking at two miles of grey elephants."

OPPOSITE, PLATE 34
Untitled (Dry Waterfall, Ghost Ranch), c. 1943
Graphite and charcoal on paper
23 7/8 x 17 7/8 in. (60.6 x 45.4 cm)
Georgia O'Keeffe Museum, Santa Fe, N. Mex. Gift of The Burnett Foundation
CR 1071

Notes

1. Sheila Tryk, "O'Keeffe," *New Mexico Magazine*, Jan.–Feb. 1973, 19.

2. Willa Cather, *Death Comes for the Archbishop* (London: William Heinemann Ltd., 1936), 5.

3. Georgia O'Keeffe to Dorothy Brett, April 1930, in Jack Cowart, Juan Hamilton, and Sarah Greenough, *Georgia O'Keeffe: Art and Letters* (Washington, D.C.: National Gallery of Art; New York: New York Graphic Society Books and Little, Brown, 1987), letter 53.

4. Amei Wallach, "Under a Western Sky," *Horizon* 20 (Dec. 1977): 26.

5. Tryk, "O'Keeffe," 19.

6. Georgia O'Keeffe, *Georgia O'Keeffe* (1976; reprint, New York: Penguin Books, 1985), text accompanying pl. 59.

7. Henry Seldis, "Georgia O'Keeffe at 78," *Los Angeles Times "West" Magazine*, 22 Jan. 1967, 14.

Sources for the Marginal Quotations

PAGE 78
Taylor, "Lady Dynamo—Miss O'Keeffe, Noted Artist Is a Feminist," *New York World Telegram*, 31 Mar. 1945, sec. 2, p. 9.

PAGE 80
Georgia O'Keeffe to Russell Hunter, Aug. 1931, *Georgia O'Keeffe: Art and Letters*, letter 57.

PAGE 84
Georgia O'Keeffe to Alfred Stieglitz, 20 Sept. 1937, in *Georgia O'Keeffe: Catalogue of the 14th Annual Exhibition of Paintings with Some Recent O'Keeffe Letters*, exh. cat. (New York: An American Place, 1937).

PAGE 87
Robert Hughes, "Loner in the Desert," *Time*, 12 Oct. 1970, 64.

A SENSE OF PLACE II

CHAMA RIVER

WHITE PLACE

ABIQUIU

GHOST RANCH

CHAMA
RIVER

OPPOSITE, PLATE 35

Chama River, Ghost Ranch,
N. Mex., 1934/1935
Oil on canvas
30 x 16 in. (76.2 x 40.6 cm)
Private collection
CR 851

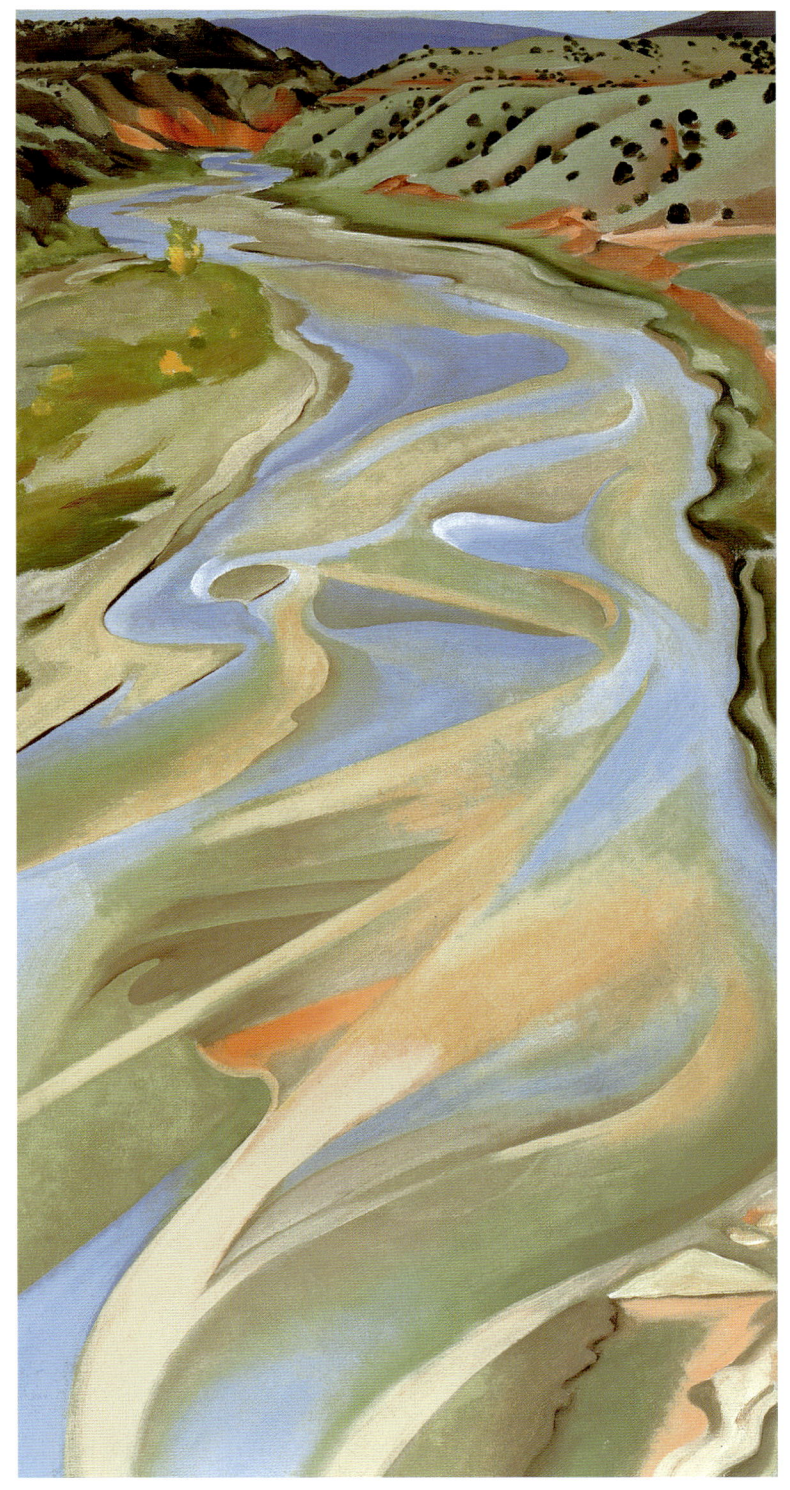

WHITE
PLACE

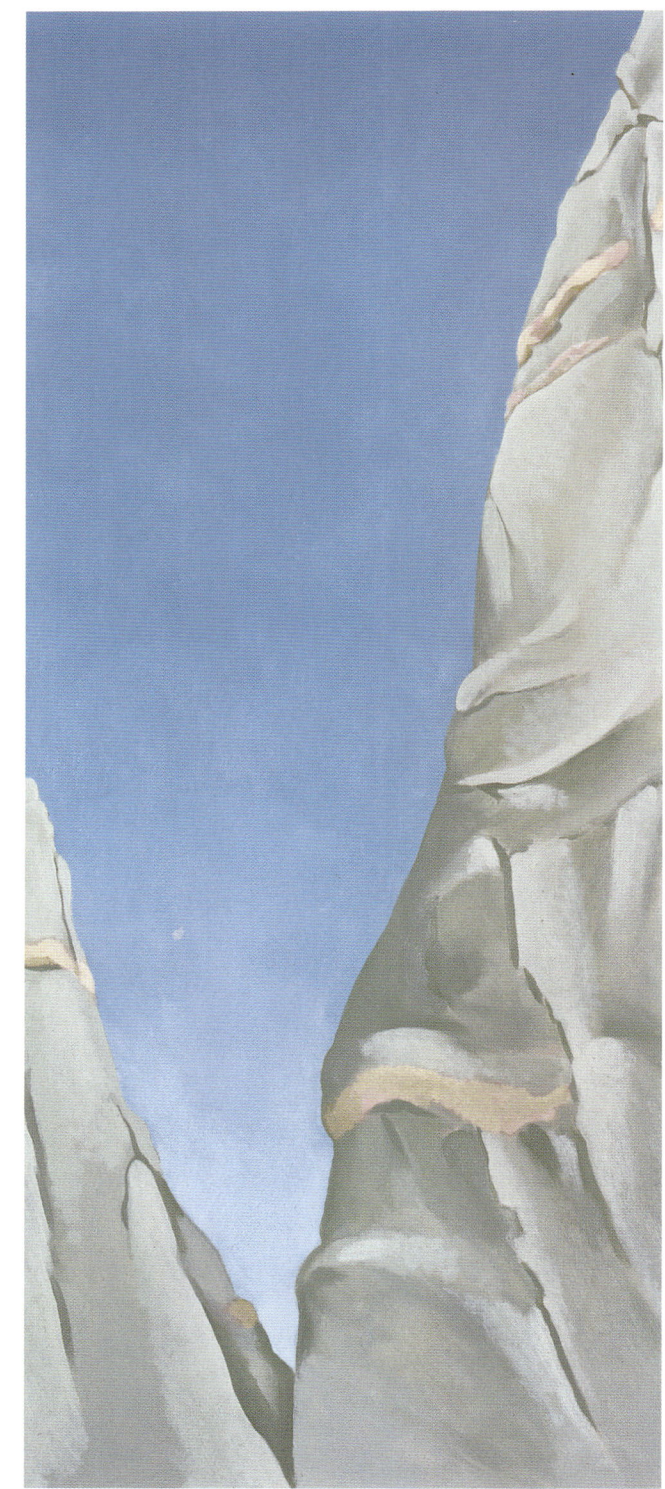

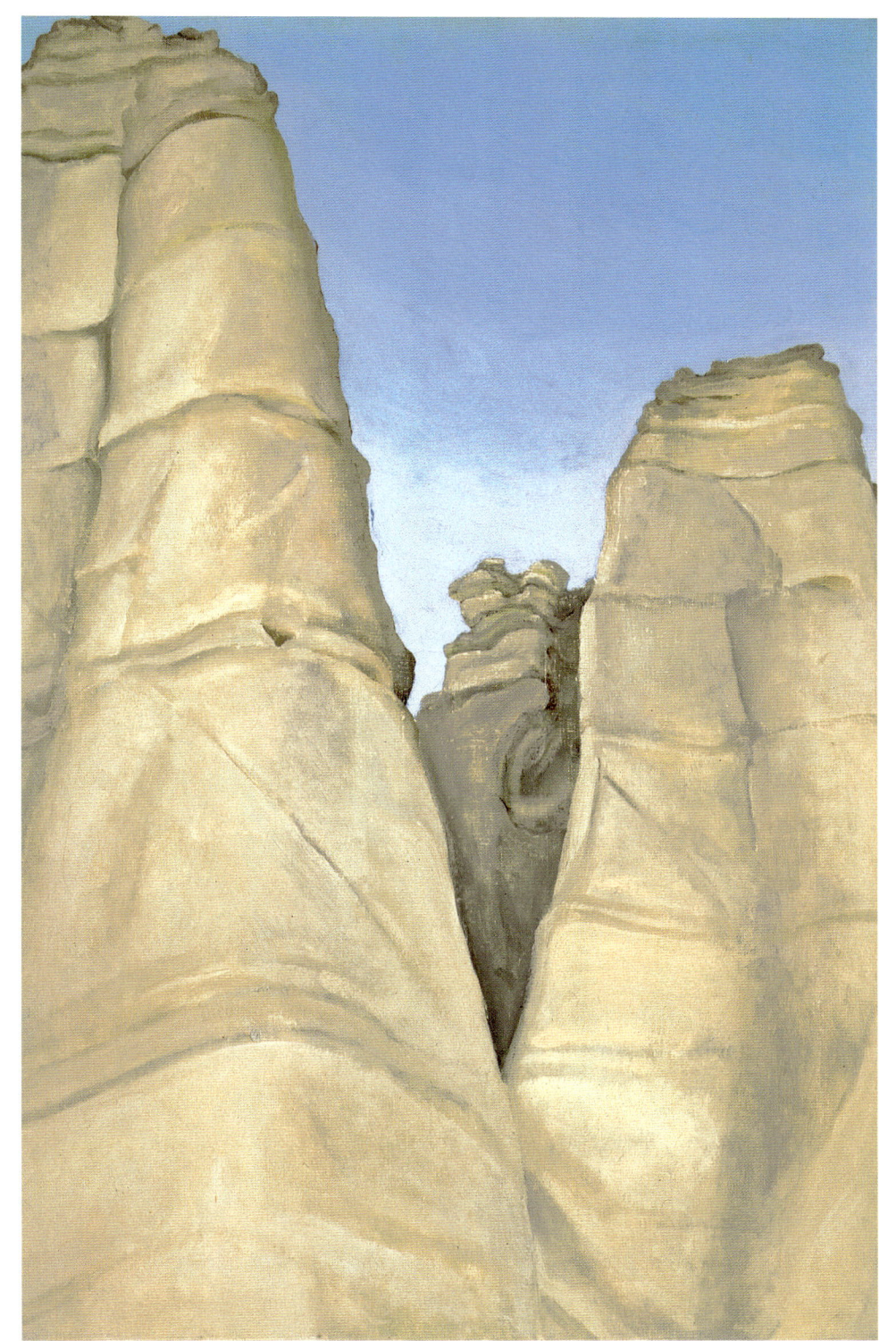

ABIQUIU

RIGHT, PLATE 38
The Mountain, New Mexico, 1931
Oil on canvas
30 x 36 in. (76.2 x 91.4 cm)
Whitney Museum of American
Art, New York. Purchase 32.14
CR 790

OPPOSITE, PLATE 39
Red Hills Beyond Abiquiu, 1930
Oil on canvas
30 x 36 in. (76.2 x 91.4 cm)
Eiteljorg Museum of American
Indians and Western Art,
Indianapolis
CR 743

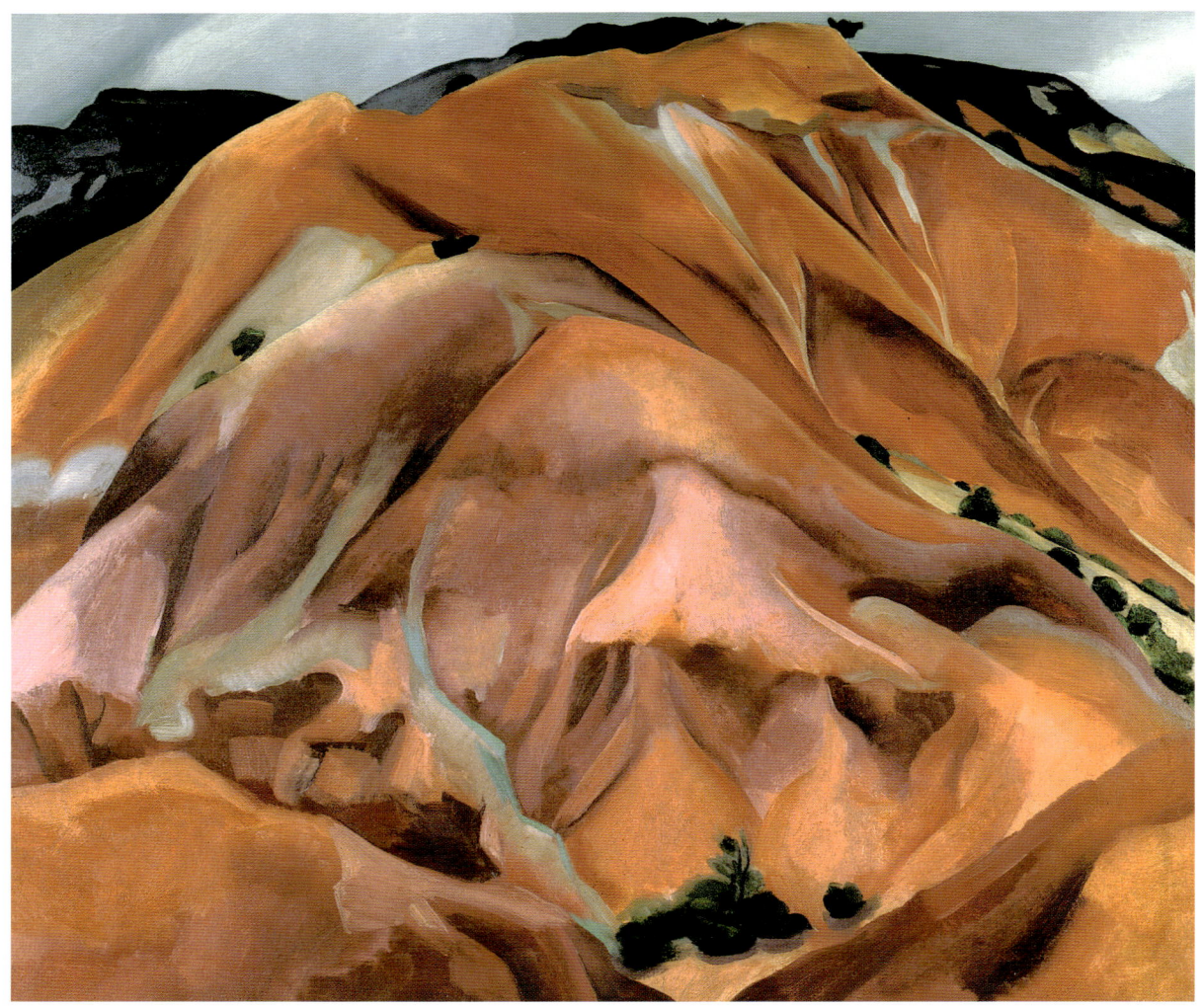

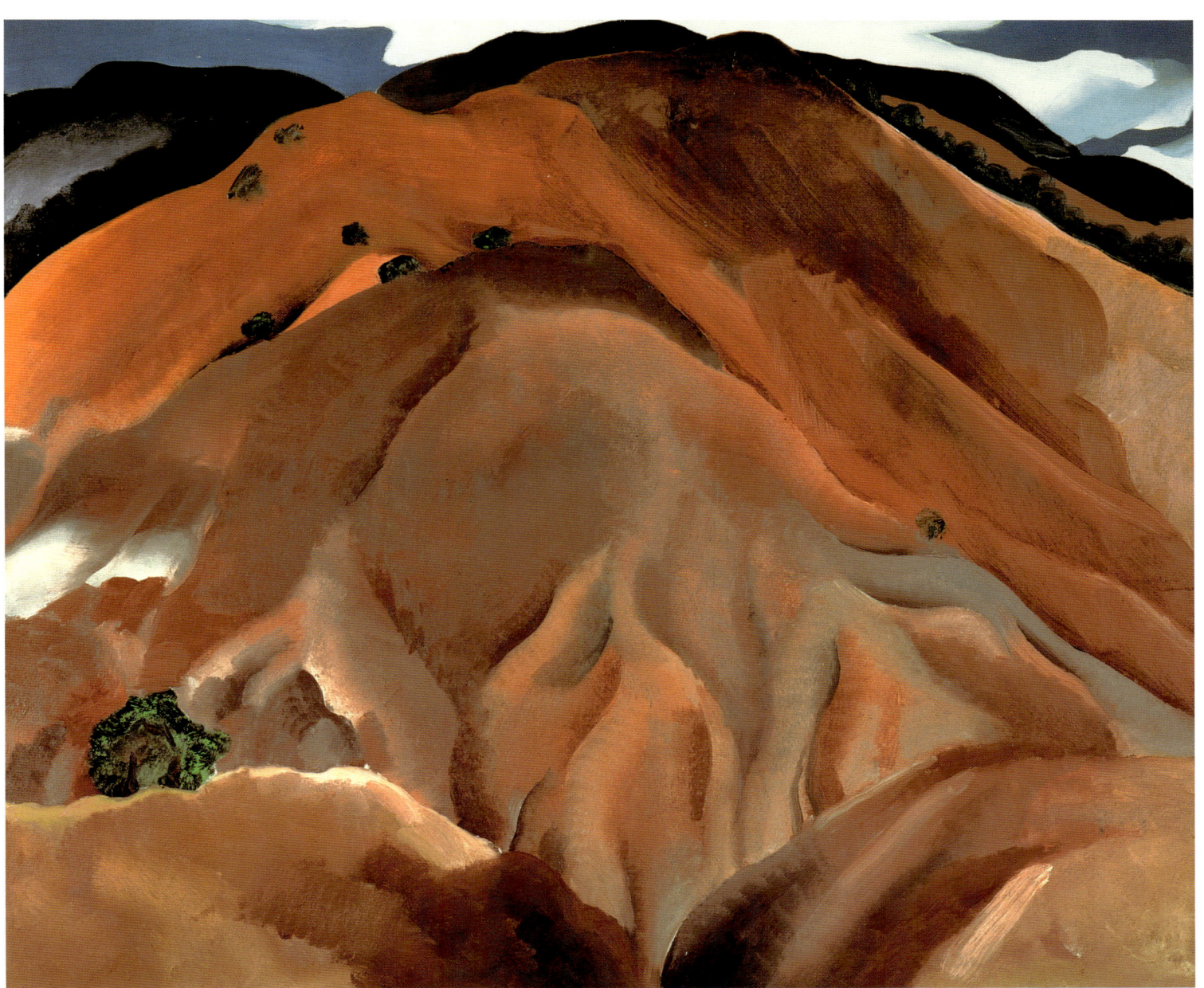

GHOST
RANCH

Red Hills and White Flower, 1937
Pastel on paper
19 3/8 x 25 5/8 in. (74.6 x 65.1 cm)
Georgia O'Keeffe Museum,
Santa Fe, N. Mex. Gift of
The Burnett Foundation
CR 925

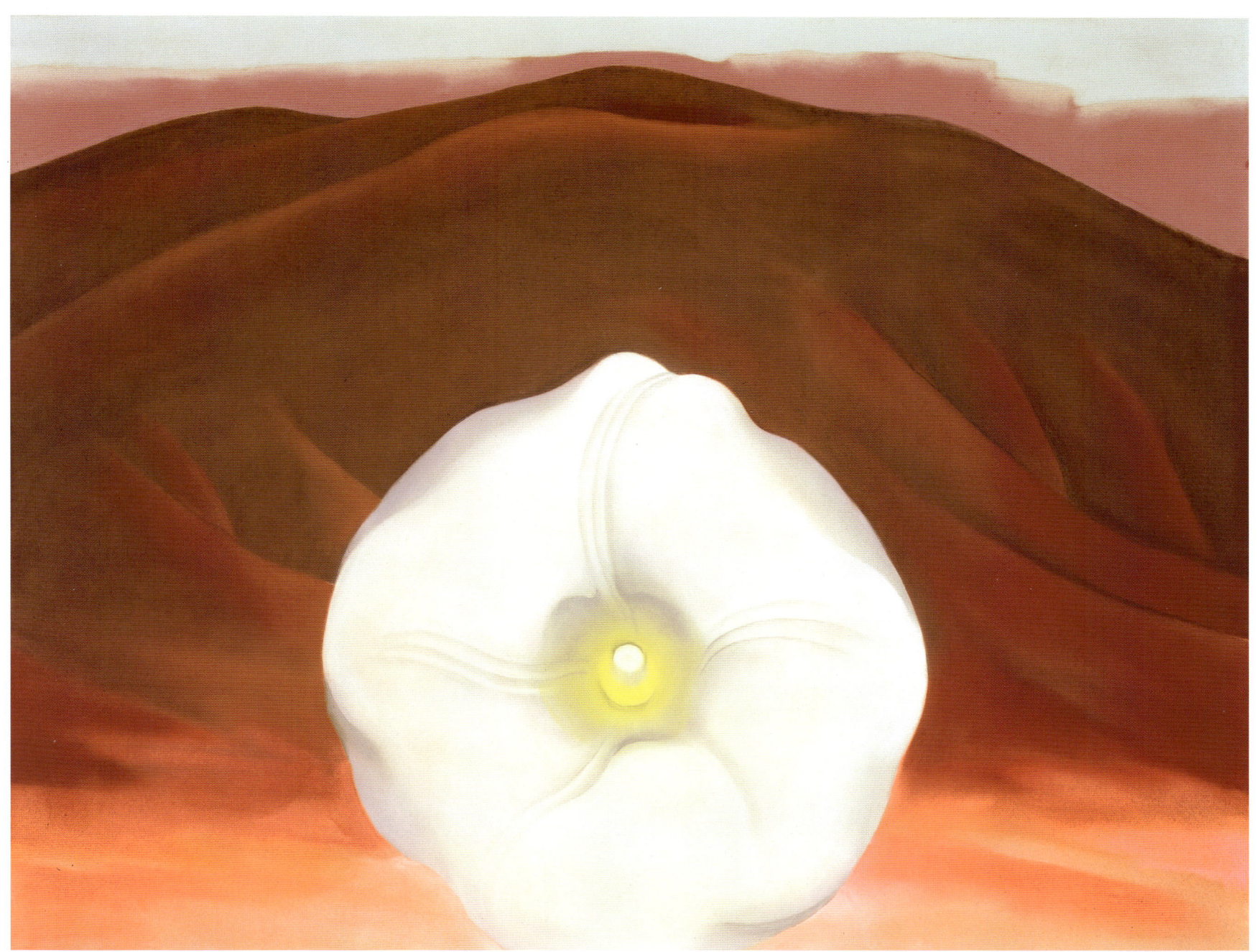

RIGHT, PLATE 41
Pedernal, New Mexico, 1936
Oil on canvas
10 1/8 x 12 1/8 in. (25.7 x 30.8 cm)
Private collection
CR 901

OPPOSITE, PLATE 42
Red Hills with Pedernal,
White Clouds, 1936
Oil on canvas
20 x 30 in. (50.8 x 76.2 cm)
Private collection
CR 899

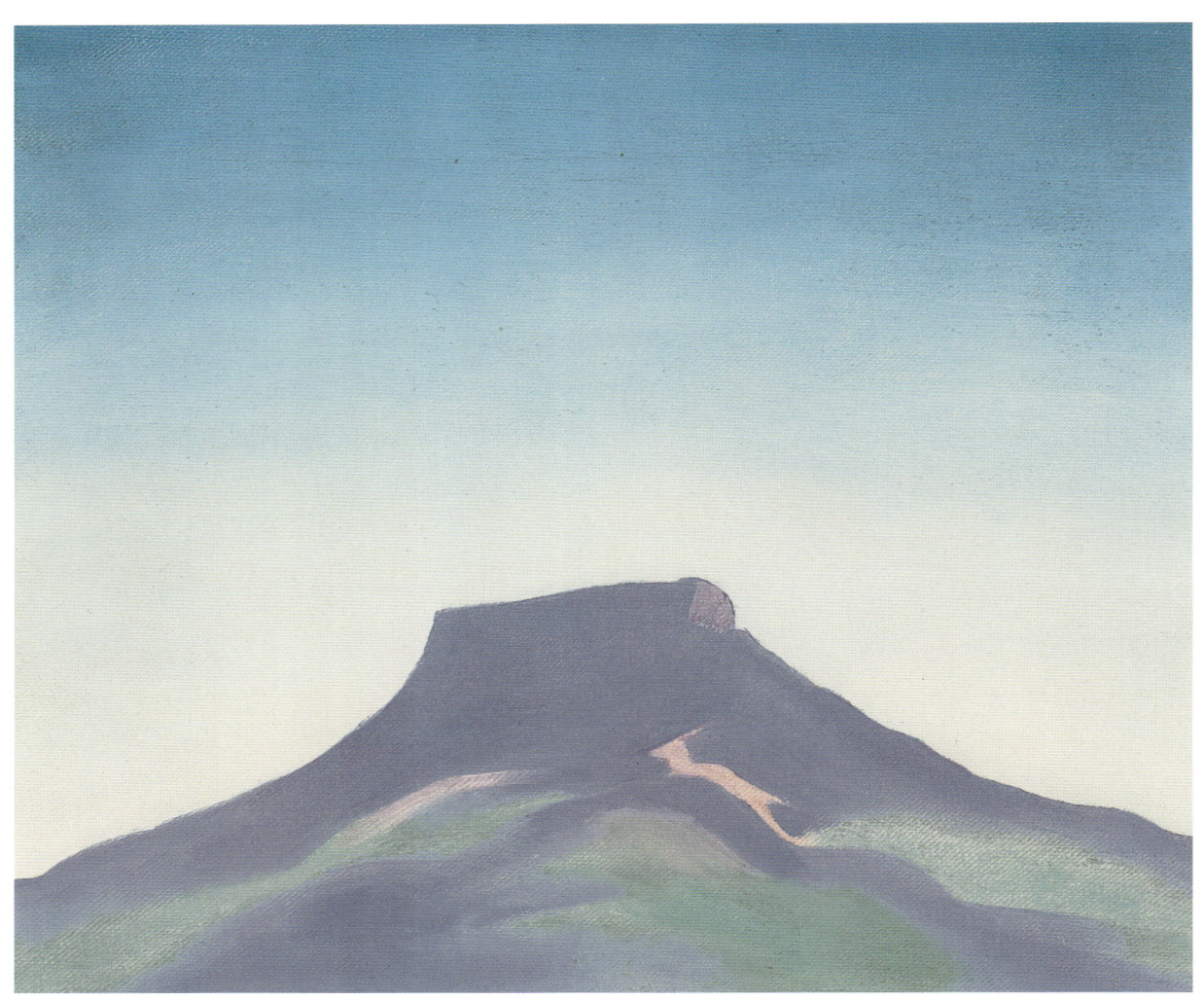

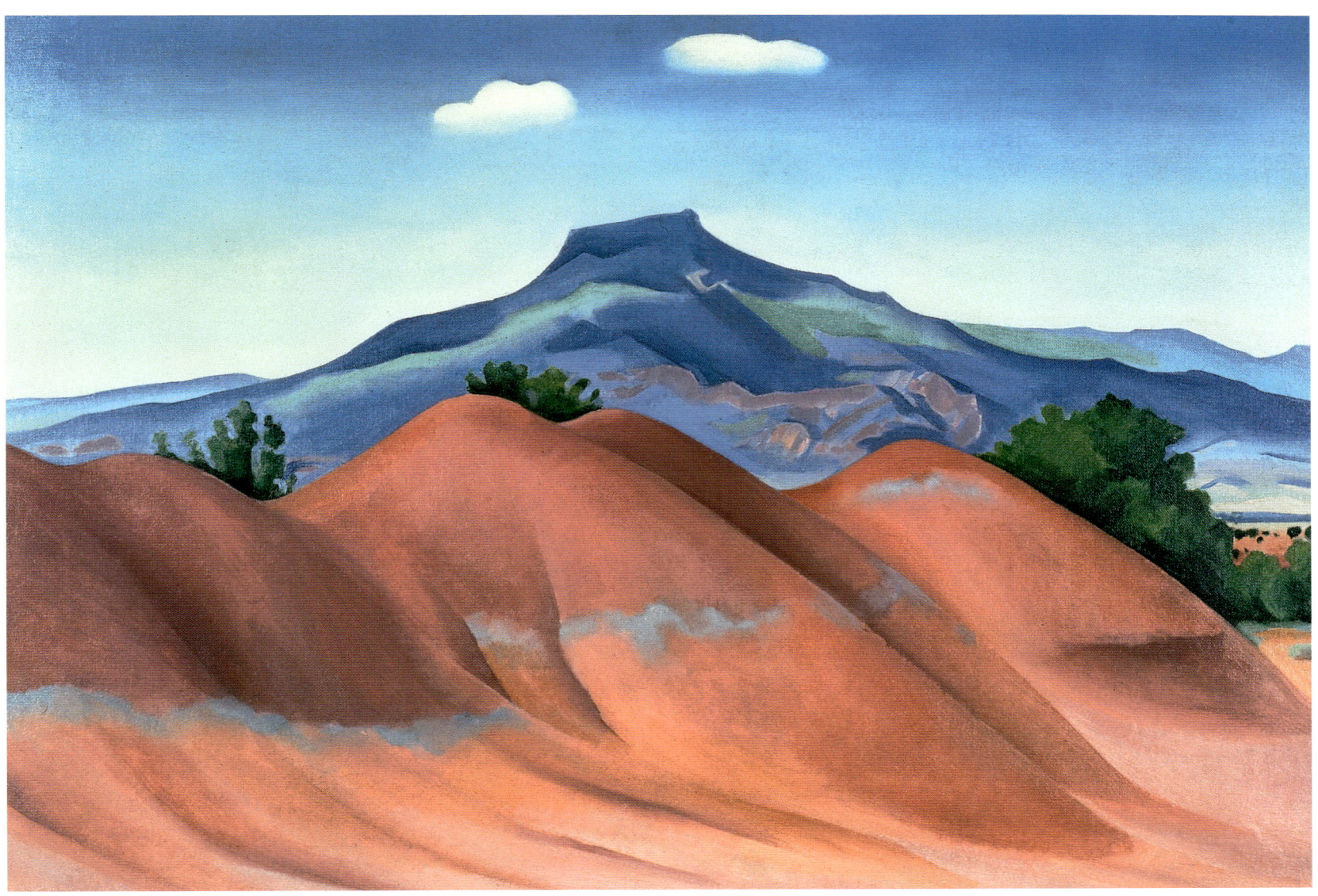

RIGHT, PLATE 43

Red Hills, Blue Sky, 1937
Oil on canvas
9 x 14 in. (22.9 x 35.6 cm)
Herbert F. Johnson Museum
of Art, Cornell University,
Ithaca, N.Y. Dr. and Mrs. Milton
Lurie Kramer (Class of 1936)
Collection: Bequest of Helen
Kroll Kramer
CR 927

OPPOSITE, PLATE 44

Red Hills No. I—
New Mexico, 1937
Oil on canvas
16 x 36 in. (40.6 x 91.4 cm)
Bedford Family Collection
CR 928

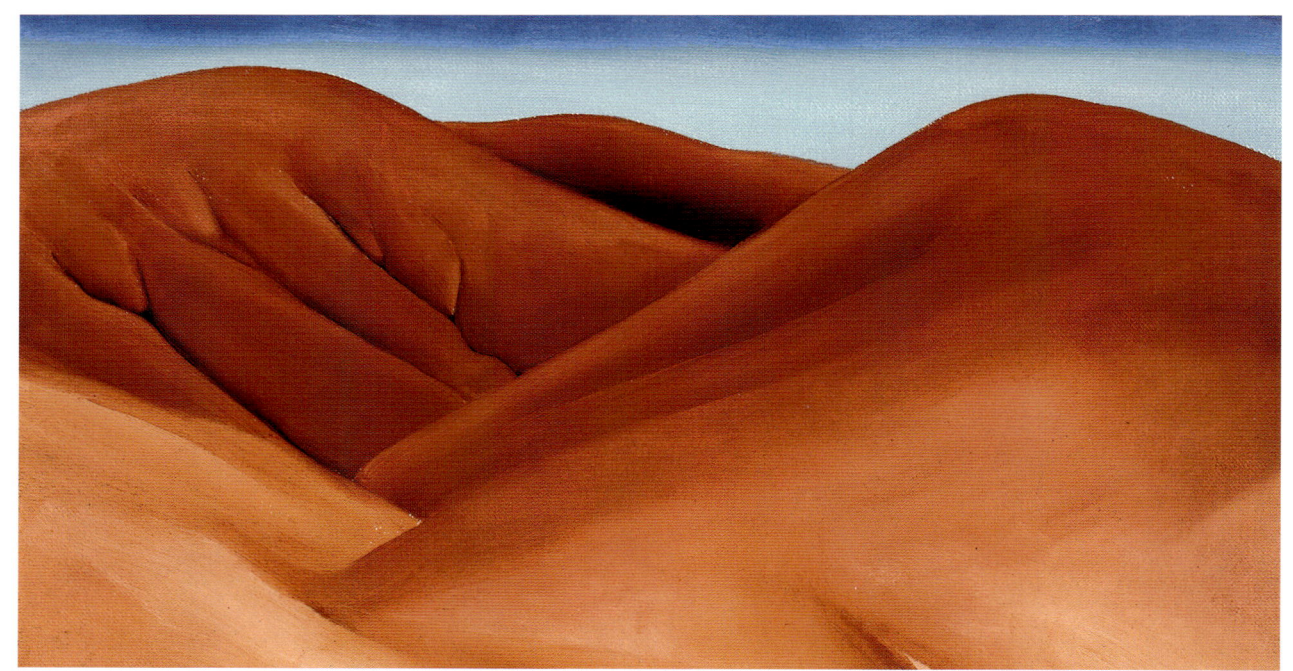

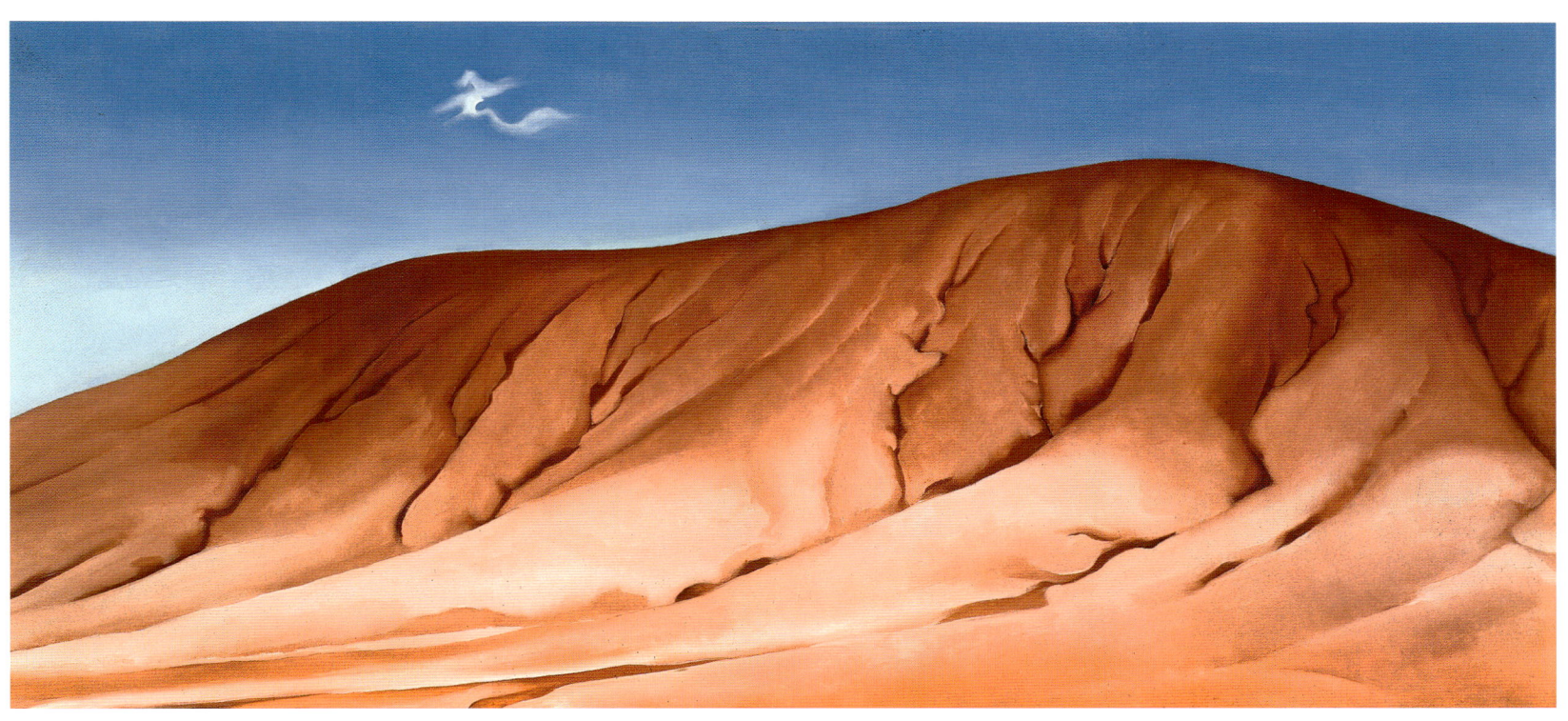

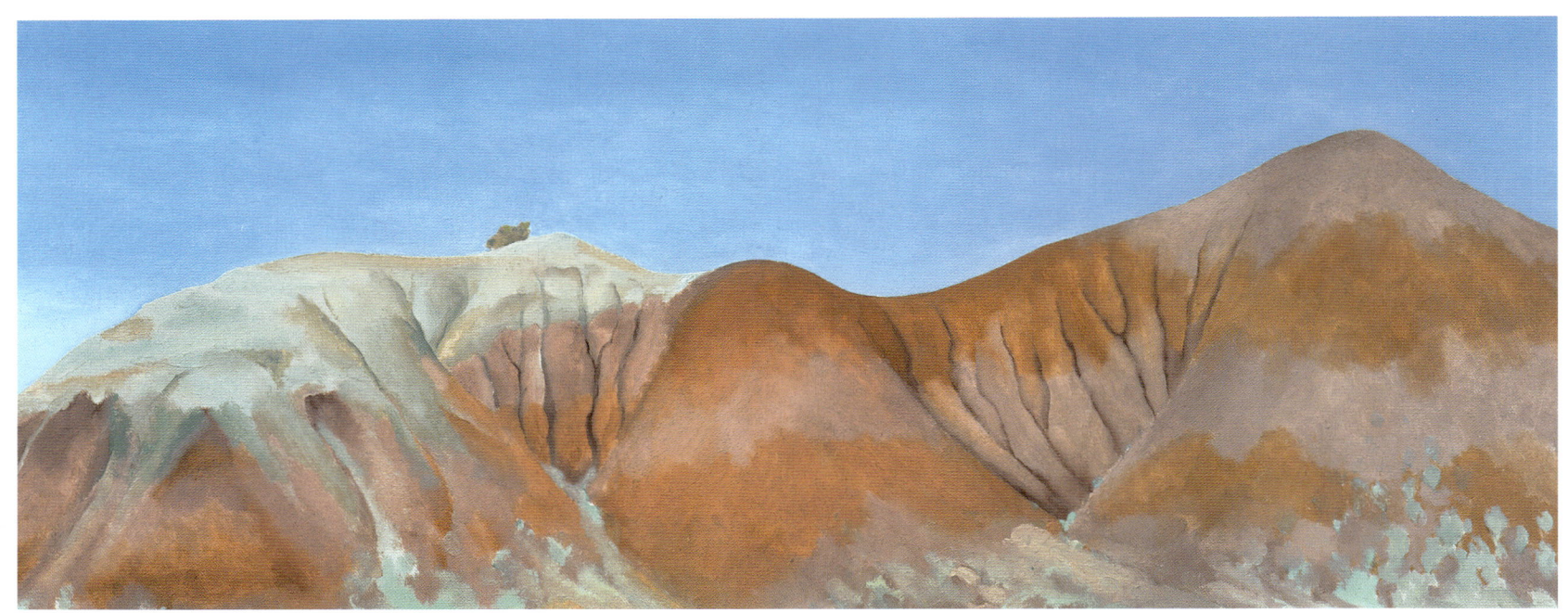

ABOVE, PLATE 45
Near Abiquiu, New Mexico, 1941
Oil on canvas
12 x 30 in. (30.5 x 76.2 cm)
Private collection
CR 1026

OPPOSITE, PLATE 46
Dry Waterfall, 1951
Oil on canvas
26 x 16 in. (66 x 40.6 cm)
Collection of Emily Fisher Landau
CR 1226

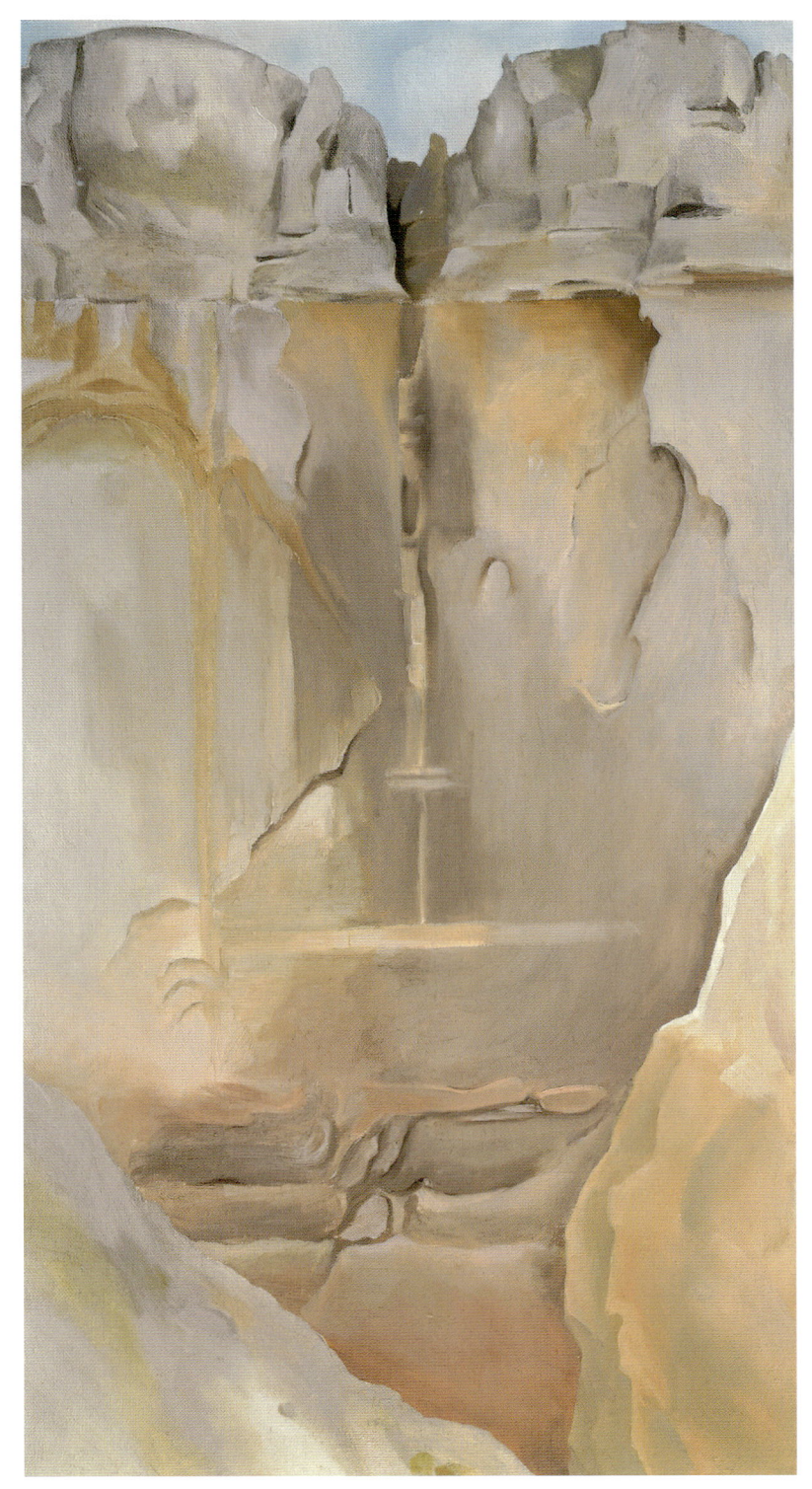

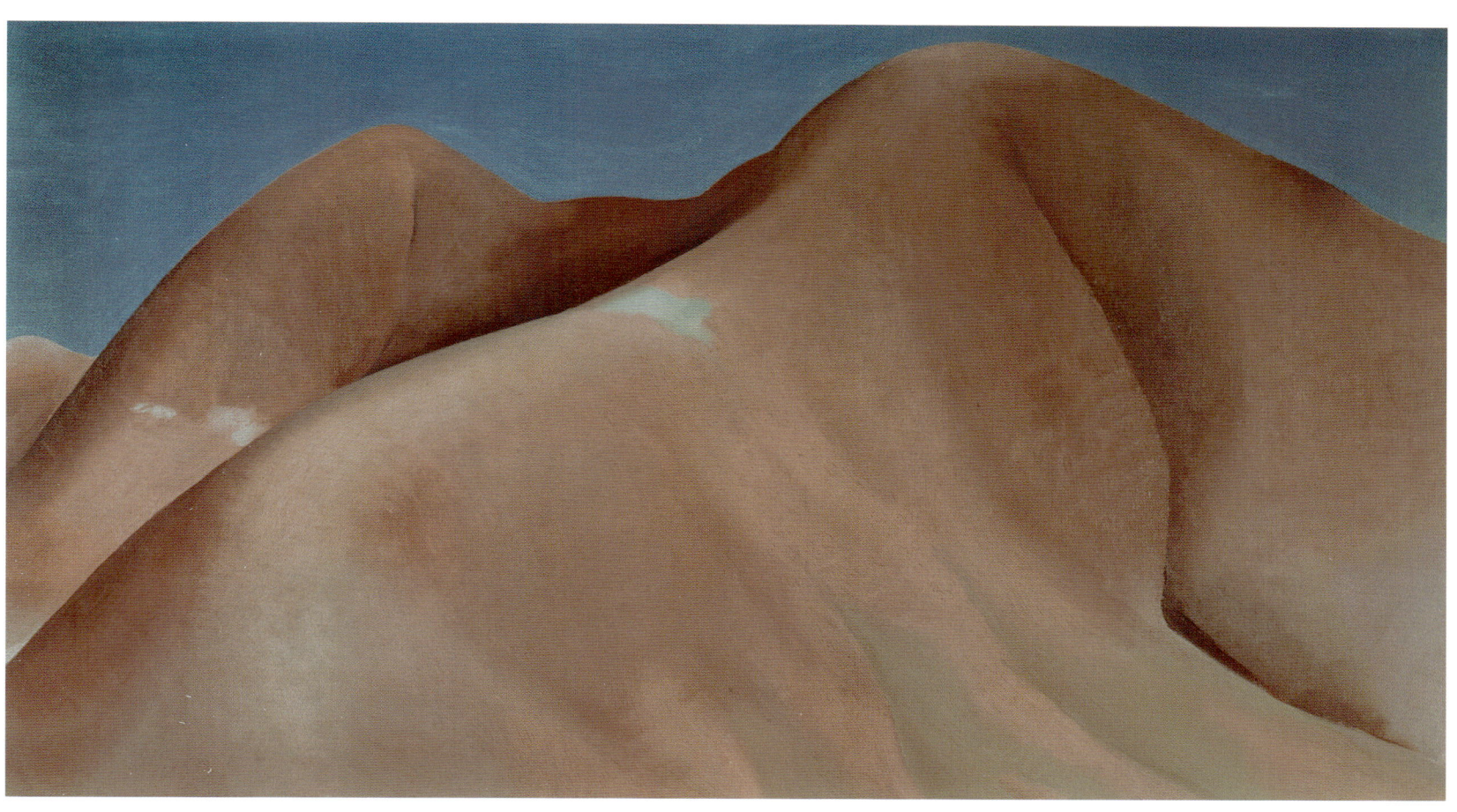

Red Hills and Bones, 1941
Oil on canvas
30 x 40 in. (76.2 x 101.6 cm)
Philadelphia Museum of Art.
Alfred Stieglitz Collection
CR 1025

OPPOSITE, PLATE 49
Stump in Red Hills, 1940
Oil on canvas
30 x 24 in. (76.2 x 61 cm)
Georgia O'Keeffe Museum,
Santa Fe, N. Mex. Gift of
The Stéphane Janssen Trust
in memory of R. Michael Johns
CR 999

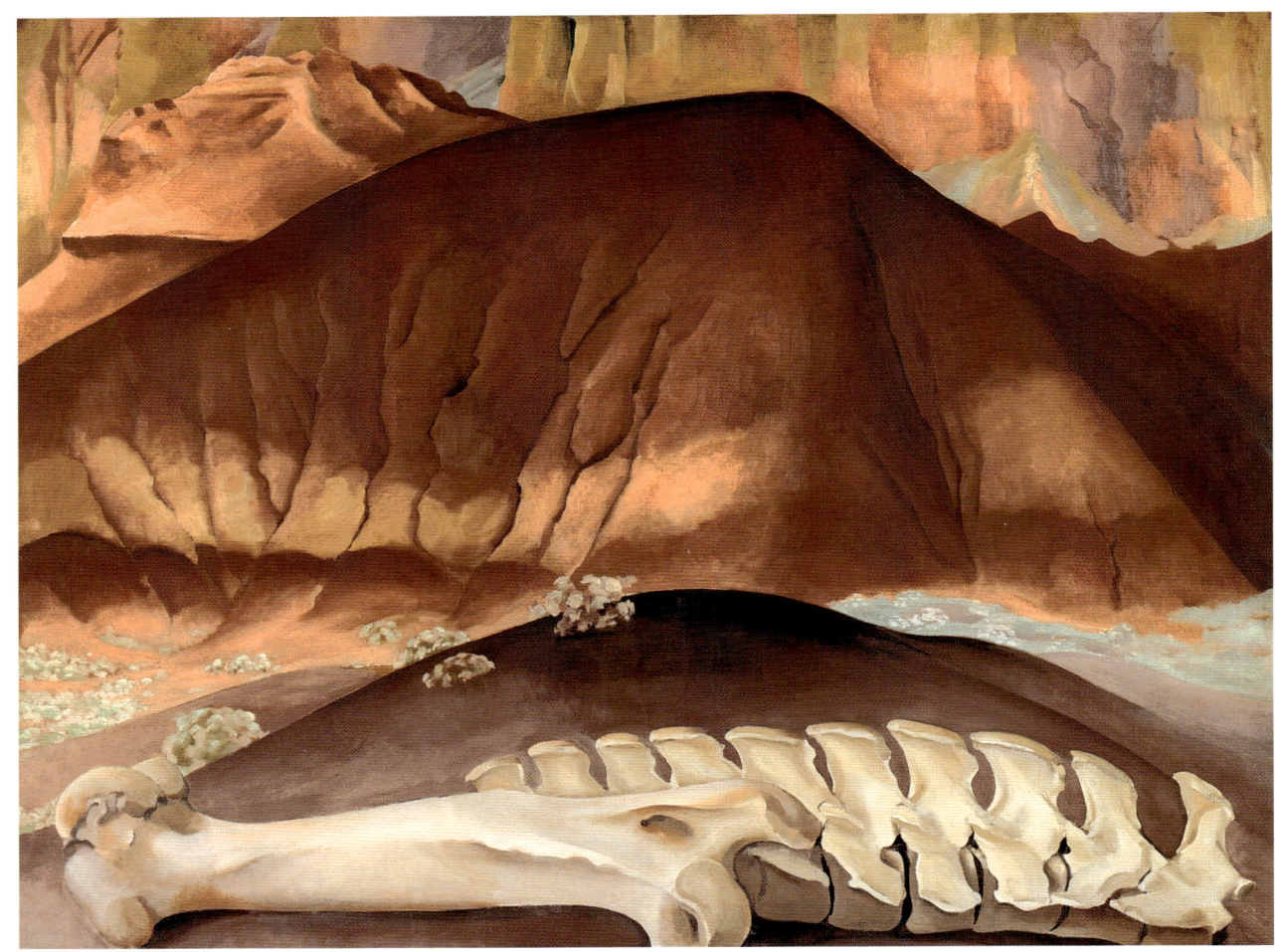

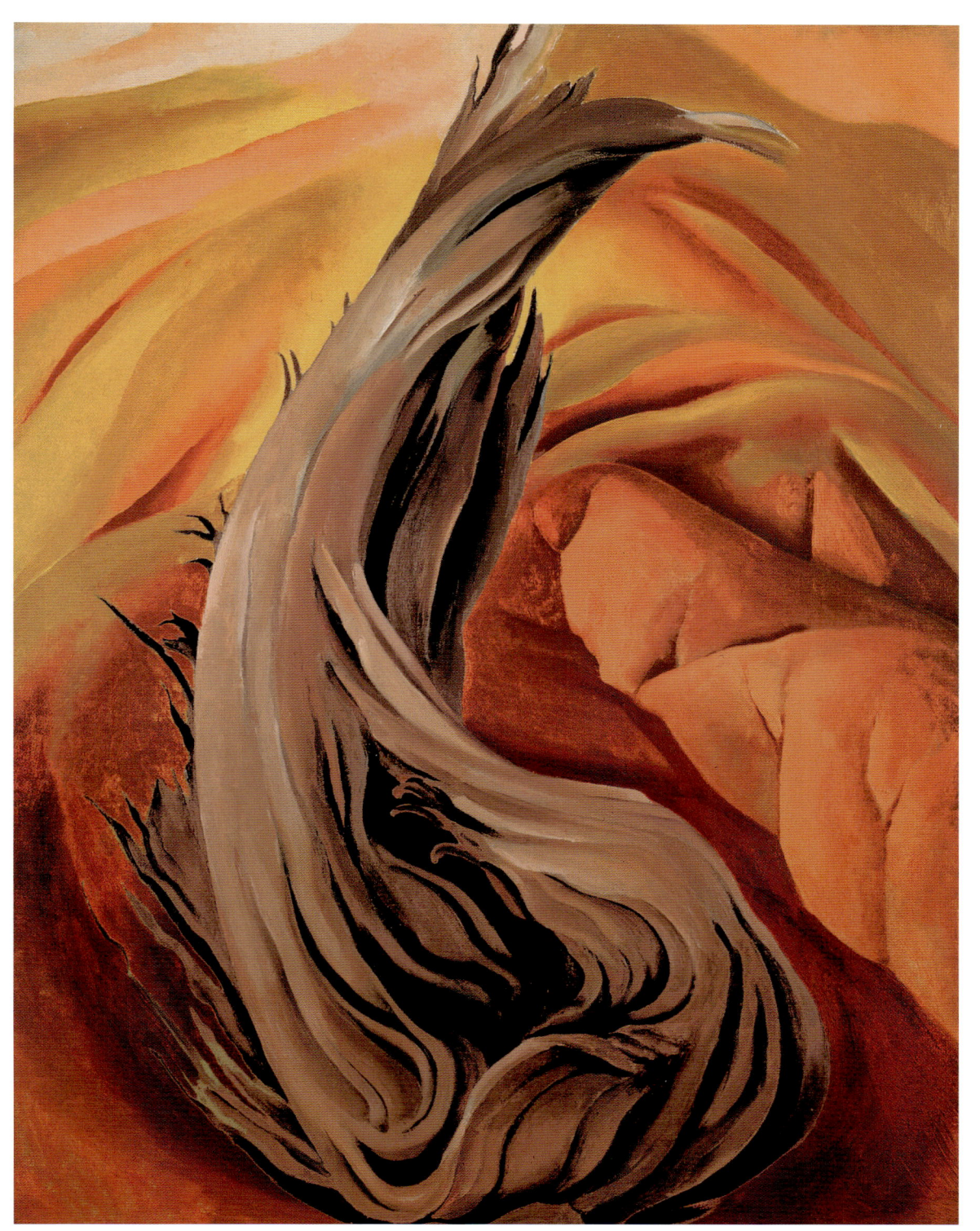

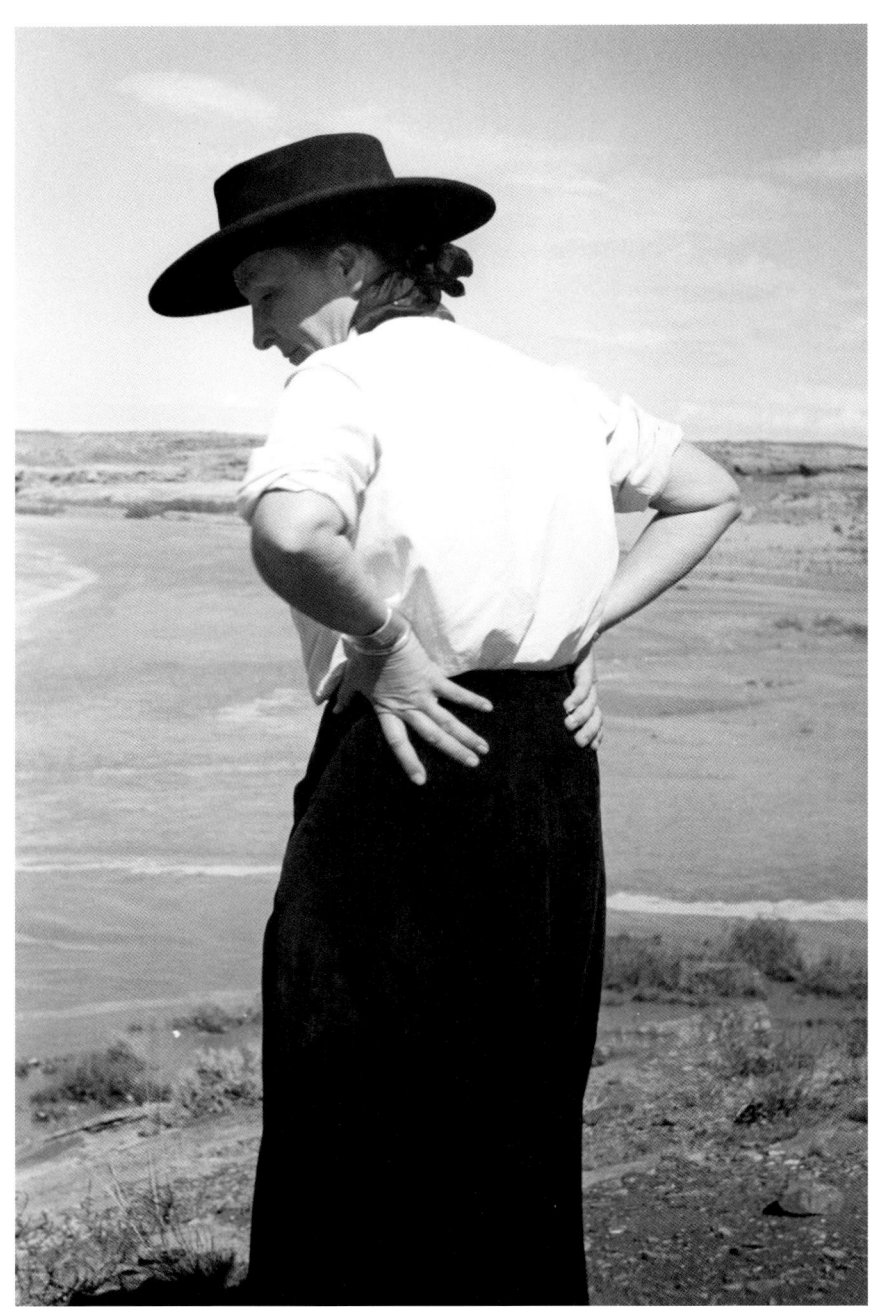

ON HER CONQUEST
OF SPACE

FREDERICK W. TURNER

WHEN MY WIFE AND I first came to Santa Fe in the mid-1970s we were given an introduction to the painters Bill and Julie James, he the grandson of the philosopher and psychologist William James. It was the beginning of a rewarding friendship, enhanced by the fact that in those days the Jameses were hosts to a large, informal salon that met frequently at their home on Old Santa Fe Trail. At the time, I don't think I quite appreciated what a distinguished group this really was or how fortunate we were to be included as marginal members of it. The photographer Eliot Porter was there with his wife, Aline, a painter. So were John Brinkerhoff Jackson, then the most prominent critic and historian of the national landscape, and Edward Hall, the noted anthropologist. The artist Agi Sims and her companion, Mary Lou Aswell, were regulars. Aswell was the literary editor who had discovered Eudora Welty, and when Welty visited in the summers, she, too, came out to the Jameses'. I met the novelist John Masters there several times. The next-door neighbors were the noted collectors and patrons of modern American art Gifford and Joanne Phillips, and on New Year's Eve we would meet at their house for a champagne session.

This was a lively, intense group, brimming with ideas and opinions, and one of the things I found most stimulating about it was that the members knew their regional and local history. Almost all of them had come to New Mexico from elsewhere—though not recently—but they had taken the

OPPOSITE, FIG. 22
Ansel Adams, *Georgia O'Keeffe*, 1937

time to learn a lot about the beautiful, slightly exotic place they now called home. For me, being around them was the equivalent of getting an immersion course in Southwestern history—and a lot of great food and wine to go along with it. Worse things have happened.

The point of this brief autobiographical excursion is that in all those many gatherings I never recall so much as a mention of Georgia O'Keeffe.

There was plenty of talk, some of it quite spirited, about art, books, film, politics. There was talk about the younger generation of Native American artists coming up—T.C. Cannon, Doug Hyde, Dan Namingha, Kevin Red Star. I recall a discussion of poet Haniel Long's brilliant interlinear to the narrative of Cabeza de Vaca and whether this was a contribution to history or a meddling in it. I remember a consideration of the Cinco Pintores and whether they had done lasting damage to art in Santa Fe with what someone called their "blue sky school of painting." But never any talk of Georgia O'Keeffe.

At the time this didn't strike me as peculiar. I was, after all, a newcomer and probably more callow than my years could account for, and so it was only after O'Keeffe had moved to a secluded home known as Sol y Sombra (Sun and Shadow) just a few hundred yards down the road from the Jameses that I thought about it at all. By that point my wife and I were living directly across the road from them, and one evening when it was just the four of us at supper I asked them if they knew O'Keeffe at all or had seen her since she had become our neighbor. "We saw her—once," Bill said. "Years ago. It wasn't very pleasant." They'd been on some sort of outing north of town, Julie amplified, when they'd encountered an old friend who had O'Keeffe with her. The artist had kept her distance, there under the shadow of a broad-brimmed black hat, and when introduced to the Jameses had only nodded silently. As far as they knew nobody had seen anything of her since she'd moved into the house, though it was understood she was in very poor health. It was only then that I reflected, if briefly, on the silence surrounding the most famous artist in the region and one of the most famous in the entire country.

Memory is, of course, famously tricky, and it has been some years now since those salons at the Jameses'. So I called a few friends who had been part of all that to ask if my recollections were substantially accurate, and, if so, what that strange silence had meant.

"I think you are right about that," Jim Brennan told me. Jim had been a regular and a well-connected member of the Santa Fe art scene. "I don't recall Agi [Sims] or Mary Lou [Aswell] ever bringing up O'Keeffe. I don't think I even heard Eliot [Porter] talk about her, and of course, he knew her quite well. It may be we just didn't think of her as part of our world. She belonged to another world, somehow. In all those years I think I saw her only once."

Artist Sibyl Saam laughed lightly when I asked her about O'Keeffe. "Well," she said, "she wasn't exactly handing out directions to her house, was she? She had very strict rules about that sort of thing. I guess we thought of her as, oh, *formidable*."

Gifford and Joanne Phillips knew virtually everybody in contemporary American art circles but had met O'Keeffe only twice, and never in Santa Fe. Once was at the San Francisco Museum of Modern Art. "She was re-hanging a show a friend of ours had just hung," Joanne remembered (something for which O'Keeffe was famous). "Anyway, he introduced us and said, 'You know, Miss O'Keeffe, Mr. Phillips's uncle, Duncan Phillips, was one of your earliest collectors.' She said, 'Yes, I know. But he much preferred the boys. He liked [Arthur] Dove better.' Then she just turned away."

When I asked her about the wall of silence surrounding O'Keeffe, Joanne paused to consider. "There were a number of mysteries about her life and about her late years," she said. But these wouldn't account for all of the silence I was wondering about. "She wasn't really part of the Santa Fe cultural scene, except for the Chamber Music Festival. She loved chamber music and was very generous to them. She wasn't part of the New York art scene, either. She'd come out here in part to get away from all that. She was really a woman apart."

And yet, if there was this wall of silence around O'Keeffe in those years, she was hardly neglected. She was instead a very visible presence in Santa Fe. There were, of course, all those posters of her art for sale everywhere and hanging in framed versions in homes, shops, and restaurants. Skulls of horses and cows and antlered elk were starkly mounted on whitewashed walls in tribute to her work. At an art supply store on Canyon Road there hung a framed check O'Keeffe had written for a purchase; the owner had saved it as a sacred relic. Tourist brochures spoke of the city as part of O'Keeffe country, even though it wasn't.

I think all of this—the silence and the visual tributes—was one of O'Keeffe's extraordinary creations. Part of it probably was a consequence of a sort of notoriety, as Joanne Phillips had suggested. There were those beautifully erotic photographs Alfred Stieglitz had taken of her back in the New York days and that followed her, even after her appearance had so dramatically changed and she'd become something of a severely dressed desert anchorite. And then there were those famously strict rules the artist successfully enforced about her contacts with the rest of the world: These were always to be exclusively on her chosen terms.

But beyond any of this, beyond the whiff of notoriety, the rumors, eccentricities, reclusiveness, caginess, there was something else at work here. The force of her *intent* was so great, her *will* to take creative possession of a particular place so powerful, that through the long years of her struggle and achievement it created a special sort of space around her. Perhaps, even early on, she had known it would. Writing to novelist Jean Toomer in 1926, she looked down the winding road that would end in the red rock country of northern New Mexico and saw "aloneness—not because I wish it so but because there seems no other way." Like another famous American solitary, Henry David Thoreau, she had business to transact with nature, and it could only be done by one.

If you're trying to write about art, hanging around with practicing painters can save you from committing some fatuous mistakes to paper—though nobody can save you from all of them. I had been wanting to make a pilgrimage to O'Keeffe country, to view the scenes of her unique conquest, and

I thought it might be helpful to do so with my old friends Sam Scott and Eugene Newmann, both well-known painters and longtime residents of Santa Fe. Sam had run watercolor workshops out of Ghost Ranch for many years and knew the country intimately. As an inheritor of the influence of the Abstract Expressionists, Gene had his own carefully reasoned aesthetic attitude toward O'Keeffe and wasn't shy about articulating it. So, we set off from Santa Fe on a blustery, changeful March first, which seemed to us the first day of spring. The sky to the north looked dark, and it was clearly snowing in portions of the Jemez Mountains to the west. Sam thought the characteristic colors of O'Keeffe country might be changed by a snowfall, but we'd take our chances with that.

Like some others I'd asked about O'Keeffe, both men had had but a single sighting of her—Sam remembering the timbre of her voice, and Gene recalling he'd heard that voice raised in Santa Fe's Fine Arts Museum as O'Keeffe berated someone for a promise that hadn't been fulfilled. On the main drag of the village of Espanola, the throbbing of a low-rider's stereo system next to us at a light prompted talk of her somewhat uneasy relationship with the locals around Abiquiu, almost all of them Hispanic. She had carefully defined the terms of that relationship, too, had never learned Spanish, and had essentially limited her interactions to practical matters. There she was through the decades, in their midst, painting their lands, yet clearly determined to remain a "woman apart." Even so, there were incidents of her spontaneous generosity, both to individuals and the community, and so who could say what the balance sheet finally looked like—except that it certainly bore her signature?

Past Espanola the roadside looked almost stunningly blighted by poverty under the now-bleak light and with winter's snows gone from the fields. The poverty would long have been here and, to judge from Farm Security Administration photographs, might have been even more desperate when O'Keeffe came up here in the Depression years. But now there was an imperishability to much of the detritus of that poverty, and both Sam and Gene wondered whether Ansel Adams could now find a frame for *Moonrise over Hernandez*, his famous 1941 photograph taken at the village we rolled past, with its junked cars, rusted agricultural implements, its tatters of plastic.

Just short of Abiquiu we turned off Route 84 onto side roads heading toward El Rito, the naked country itself taking over now. We talked about what might have drawn O'Keeffe here in the 1930s, turning her back not only on New York but even on Taos, where at least she might have had the support of its flourishing arts colony: to come here, alone, to this rugged landscape with its physical, psychological, and aesthetic demands. Was she looking for something? Or was she instead open to whatever she might encounter? Sam thought the latter. "You've gotta be *clear* when you come to this place—or any new place, really. And you don't want to sentimentalize it."

"But she did," Gene came back. He was a refugee from Nazi Europe, dried and toughened by a boyhood in Colombia where he'd worked for his father in the cowhide business, and so maybe he'd earned his cynicism—if that's what it was. He thought the central issue of O'Keeffe's work up here wasn't what she was looking for but what he termed her "relationship to the visual reference," to the landscape forms she found here and utilized. He knew her pre-Stieglitz work from Texas and South Carolina and thought that in it she'd seemed willing enough to leave the figurative references behind. But up here, he said, she'd pulled back from that edge. Sam disagreed. And I did, too, believing that what she'd found she had to do up here was to devise a strategy for taking on this power-house landscape. If there had been a retreat of sorts, it had been a strategic one that gave her a vantage point from which she might achieve some sort of parity with the landscape: stripping the bare-bones forms even further, down to their metaphysical essentials; making carefully calibrated rearrangements and simplifications; obliterating depth in her work into an almost Asian flatness. All this so that she could finally, over time, *dominate* a place she said was hers the first time she came into it. And she'd had to learn the elements of this strategy by herself. Others had shown her their techniques, and through Alon Bement she'd learned of artist Arthur Dow's ideas on Asian art. But nobody had taught her how to paint the way she found she had to out here. Even some of the techniques she'd so clearly mastered in her earlier years had to be discarded or revised in accordance with these new realities. Much seemed handed to you here—immense sky, fiery colors, fantastic shapes—but the gifts were partly illusory, fraught with dangers. She had said that the mountain in the distance seemed almost to paint itself for you—until you actually tried to do it.

Around a bend in the road, the Chama sparkling below us in a sudden spurt of sunlight, we came upon a twisted old cottonwood. "There," Gene said, "that's an O'Keeffe tree, right there." Such is the nature of her dominance of this landscape that we looked at it in silence a moment, even wondering whether it might actually be one of the cottonwoods O'Keeffe had painted in the 1950s. We parked and got out, startling into flight some Canada geese in the watery fields below the road, their long shadows low in takeoff over the fields' first and tentative green blush. While Sam did a couple of pencil sketches and Gene flipped through some color scans of O'Keeffe's paintings, I stood under the snaky arms of the old tree, trying to imagine the artist right here, on her own, as she had for some years yearned to be. In her late years she claimed she'd always been scared by her own audacity, the path-breaking risks she'd taken in painting this landscape as no one else had done. Yet, she said grimly, she'd always continued. It wasn't, I felt, a brag. The work was her proof, the validation of her courage.

The tree made me think of Willa Cather, out on the naked plains of southernmost Nebraska where, if she could find in some sandy draw a scabby cottonwood like this one, she could feel some visual relief from the relentless monotony of grass and sky. Her story was the reverse image of O'Keeffe's: ripped from her Virginia roots and stuck down into the soil of the Great West—which she left behind as soon as she was able. Thereafter, Cather created fictional variations on a central theme: the artistic soul stranded in Nowheresville and struggling to find some means of self-expression. Out here, however, O'Keeffe found the barren land releasing energies and creative impulses that had been dormant in her New York years.

It was noon by now, and our spot above the river a beauty, and we thought about opening a bottle of wine we'd packed along with our picnic supplies. We decided against it: Possibly it would sharpen our response to the visual opportunities awaiting us, but then it might dull us as well. Ernest Hemingway, I told my friends, claimed that the art of looking was enhanced by hunger, and so we went on, following the sign for the Dar Al-Islam Foundation up the red, rutted road with the sagebrush spilling away on either side, scrubby, tough, irregular. Then, suddenly, we were at the White Place, and here the spoken surmises of three garrulous men surrendered to the bizarre, blanched luminescence of this place of mud and ash, mounded up in minarets as if it had been the playground of the children of the higher powers.

We sat in silence before it, each of us, I thought, awed by the look of the place itself and mentally making the comparisons with O'Keeffe's renderings of it. The March wind drove the clouds quickly overhead, changing the color values from moment to moment. Sam wanted to try a watercolor, and while he did that I took some notes. After Sam had finished and we'd turned back down the road, I had the distinct feeling of my friends' silent assent to the nobility of their fellow artist's effort here. They knew, as I could not, the intimate nature of that effort, the solitary engagement between artist and landscape—Jacob and the angel—knew what it took, knew the daily taking of risks. O'Keeffe's style was like walking out on a rocky ledge, I thought, with no room for misstep: either she would establish dominion or she'd be defeated and the paintings would be botches in which viewers wouldn't be able even to sense what she'd dared. (There are some like this, I think, but not too many.) And whatever your ultimate judgment of O'Keeffe's work might be, there could be no caviling with the profound sincerity of her engagement here, the danger in it. For her, this had been no playground.

Coming back down the road we had a fine, panoramic view of the mountains to the west, a deep bruise-blue under their cloud cover and veined with snow. Rising out of their midst was the truncated top of Pedernal, which O'Keeffe, perhaps not quite playfully, had once said God had promised to her if she remained faithful to her task of painting it often enough.

Then the picnic on the road to O'Keeffe's house beyond Ghost Ranch, looking off to the cliffs she considered part of her backyard. We had the wine now, a sturdy Côtes du Rhône, and hard-cooked eggs, salami-and-cheese sandwiches, and a South American dessert of cotijo cheese and *membrillo* (guava paste). When we'd finished we drove slowly on, and as we did I felt it again: that invisible, inviolable space O'Keeffe had created around herself and that I'd first dimly sensed at the salons on Old Santa Fe Trail more than twenty years earlier. The space was to her artistic advantage, she clearly believed, but its personal costs might eventually have proved heavier than she'd calculated. She seems to have been a loner from early on, but it is one thing to be so in youth and another to remain alone in the encroaching shadows of old age when even your great instrument, your vision, might begin to betray you.

Back on Route 84 we headed north to a spot in the red rock country that Sam wanted us to experience. The high, wind-driven drama of the day continued around us, the clouds flying overhead in quick masses. Off to the west and surrounded by sunlight there was a dense snow shower like a theophany of the Old Testament God. When we came to the red rocks—giant prows permeated with iron oxide the color of dried blood—we parked in a turnaround, got out, and waited for traffic to clear so that we could walk into the canyon opposite.

As we walked into the canyon, the gumbo mud sucked at our boots so that each step became a heavier effort. All around us were ancient twists of junipers as thick about as a man's waist. Here and there dead limbs from them lay like bones against the red mud, recalling for us O'Keeffe's *Stump in Red Hills* (plate 49) and calling to mind also her intrepid, solitary excursions through so much of this country—in the cold, wearing sweep of the wind down from Pedernal, in the blaze of summer with the sun striking off the rock faces and the bees swarming around her ears. In this latter season, far away from her house, her only shelter from the sun might be the oily shade underneath her car.

Now that we were within the canyon proper, Sam stopped. "I just wanted you guys to see this," he said, turning around, "to *feel* it." We were surrounded by the towering craggy reaches through which, high up, there ran a rich green band of olivine so that the drama of the day was matched by the permanent drama of the rocky colors and shapes. "Here," so our situation seemed to say to us, "it is, *right here*." And then the challenge would have been what to make of "right here," with all its drama, both quotidian and ancient.

Our last stop in O'Keeffe country was Ghost Ranch. Behind its complex of buildings we walked a broad trail up into a box canyon where we came at last to a dead cottonwood shedding branches and skin in long, grey peels. "A Newmann form," Sam smiled, pointing out a forked branch caught astraddle a larger limb. "A form trying to be a form," Gene came back, and they both laughed. Through the years they had traveled and sketched and painted over a sizable stretch of earth and probably knew each other's favorite shapes about as well as they did their own. They would have understood therefore why O'Keeffe kept circling back, even in the last years, to shapes she'd been working with as long ago as those feverish nights in South Carolina when she'd drawn by the hour, sitting on the bare floor of her room.

On our way home we came to that bend of the Chama above Abiquiu where O'Keeffe had painted the river, and we pulled onto the narrow shoulder to have a quick look, as Gene and Sam were talking about John Sloan's painting, *Chama Running Red* (1925; The Anschutz Collection), with its lone horseman approaching the river and the sentinel tree on the opposite bank. It was, they said, a very narrative painting whereas O'Keeffe's was almost defiantly non-narrative. "You know," Gene said in a quiet way, "there must be very few artists who did what she did up here: to come in cold and make it your own. Pretty unusual, I'd say." As we went on we tried to come up with other examples. There was Paul Cézanne in Provence, but then he had hardly come in cold—painting his Mont Sainte-Victoire over and over again as though he, too, thought it might have been promised him for his faith. Claude Monet up in Giverny. Only two Americans came to mind: Winslow Homer up at Prout's Neck and Walter Inglis Anderson down at Ocean Springs and Horn Island on the Gulf. But Homer often escaped to the tropics in winter, while Anderson is not of O'Keeffe's stature. And these were men, men who could go where they liked, whereas she could not, as she remarked in her New York years. And up here there was the additional problem of making entry into a resolutely patriarchal culture. Who else, we wondered in spring's fickle and quick-fading light, had done what she had here?

Who else, indeed, and how?

Establishing context as a way of accounting for a work or an entire career is an inherently ham-handed effort that confesses a kind of failure as it avoids direct contact with the work. What we really want to know about a work or a career is simply stated: How the hell did she or he do it? Context can never really answer that query; the best it can do is to point out some of the materials the artist was handed by birth, background, training, and what the Germans (who specialized in this sort of thing in the nineteenth century) called Zeitgeist.

In attempting to account for O'Keeffe's singular achievement in the American West, the ground of inquiry must begin with Sun Prairie, Wisconsin. For many Europeans and for American westerners, too, this might be hard to accept, because Wisconsin is not Wyoming. Yet it is in Wisconsin's southern half that you begin to feel the gradual, gentle rolls of the valley of the great river that divides America between East and West. And in places like Sun Prairie and Baraboo, Hillsboro and La Crosse, you keep getting the ever-more-insistent sense that you're on the edge of something really big, until at last you find yourself rolling high across a bridge with the river far below—and maybe even hollering as you go, as I often have. Then on the other side, you're in the West and you can assent to the truth of the line written by a Chicago boy, poet Archibald MacLeish: "America is West and the wind blowing." O'Keeffe was brought up on that edge between the two halves of the country and heard about the land out there in the bedtime stories her mother read to the children. She was raised with the wind in her face, the wind that had gathered force in its sweep across the immense grasslands. No one so deeply sensitive as she was to landscape could have failed to register all this at some imperishable depth that was at the same time potentially accessible. When she went to New York from Texas in 1918, she was hungry and thirsty, too, for artistic and intellectual companionship, and for some years thereafter she found the city positively thrilling: You see that in her cityscapes. But she never got over the West. To her it was the real America.

In this she was deeply in what William Carlos Williams would call "the American grain." And so were those earlier great voices of the American Renaissance whose brilliance was still shining on the Modernist movement in 1918—Emerson, Thoreau, Hawthorne, Whitman—they all believed the true America lay somewhere toward the sunset, waiting to be claimed by artists courageous enough to travel beyond the eastern seaboard, with its ineradicable Old World influences. Emerson thought the outcome of the entire American experiment might depend on what was done out there. Thoreau claimed that whenever he went for a saunter his steps inevitably tended westward, toward the future. And Whitman, the great singer of New York, believed that the West was where America's true songs would be expressed, its authentic images made. "Do you term that perpetual, pistareen, paste-pot work American art?" he rhetorically asked in *Democratic Vistas*. "I think I hear, echoed as from some mountain-top afar in the west, the scornful laugh of the Genius of these States."

Who can say definitively how much of this O'Keeffe absorbed? In her New York days she was evidently careful not to reveal too much to "the boys" about what she was thinking, what she might have been reading, what portions of the all-but-endless, high-flown talk about modern American art, the Great American Novel, an American epic poem, she actually attended. Indeed, she was so secretive in this way that one member of the Stieglitz circle later expressed surprise that she could actually read and write. (Still later, of course, as she set about the earnest work of building her legend, she was very careful to cover her tracks, making it appear she'd created herself out of sunlight, dust, and rock.) When she got tired of all the twaddle, she said, she simply left the table. But there is no doubt she knew her intellectual history, was keenly aware of the tenor of her times. And she knew, too, that the talk around Stieglitz provided a vital, countervailing force to the riptide that was bearing some of America's brightest talents back to the Old World, especially to Paris. Later she would smugly say that the whole bunch—Dove, John Marin, Marsden Hartley, Paul

Strand, Charles Demuth—would have gone over in a moment had it been feasible for them (Hartley and Marin had). This wasn't fair. Yet Ezra Pound, Gertrude Stein, Hemingway, Edward Hopper, Malcolm Cowley, and Virgil Thomson had all gone, and the social critic Harold Stearns had claimed that artists had to leave America or else risk being stifled by the permanent strain of Puritanism in the native culture.

One voice of Modernism O'Keeffe must have heard with especial clarity was that of Stieglitz's good friend, the doctor from across the river in New Jersey, William Carlos Williams. Stieglitz had loved Williams's book *In the American Grain*, and in calling his gallery An American Place, Stieglitz was seemingly acknowledging Williams's influence. The year previous, Williams, too, had tried the expatriate life but found he was unsuited for it. He was too American. Writing to the critic Kenneth Burke near the end of his stay abroad, Williams said Paris would be a wonderful place to live and write if only he were French. But since he wasn't, "Only America remains where at least I was born."

"Where at least I was born." That was the challenge, the problem for artists, writers, musicians from the beginnings here. Being born in this huge sprawl of a country that seemed bereft of accessible traditions or history, how to come in cold, as Gene Newmann had put it, and make it your own. Williams's decision had been to take on the severely local Paterson, New Jersey—its mills and exhausted landscape—and hammer an epic out of it. Others were trying to take on New York and its soaring modernities, which Europeans like Marcel Duchamp thought so rich in potential. O'Keeffe was one of them. And still others began to make tentative forays into the imponderable spaces of the West, following the outsized blazes of Karl Bodmer, Albert Bierstadt, and Thomas Moran. Looking at the work of William Robinson Leigh, Walter Ufer, Hartley, and Marin, you see just how imponderable those spaces really were for them.

Western spaces were also a problem for a woman born on the edge of the West. But she at least had grown up with Western grit in her teeth and had learned finally that this could be a kind of nourishment in disguise. In the West Texas dirt country in 1916 she often came home covered with the blowing dirt and later spoke of that as if it had been a blessing—as in truth it was for her. She wanted to feel that Western earth in all its spareness, its mercilessness. Why else, you think, did she take those teaching posts way out there, so far from any other source of nurture and inspiration, except for the fact that she understood, however obscurely, that the West could be her mother lode? There was something about the sun in the West that drew her, something about the way it hit the naked land, burning deep into it, and in *No. 21—Special* (fig. 23), she got that in paint, with shapes resembling molten boulders rumbling out of the canyon's clarified curves. *No. 21—Special* is an earnest of what she would go on to do in northern New Mexico, even if in painting it she could not quite see that yet.

Between *No. 21—Special* and her first summer in New Mexico lay thirteen years in New York and Lake George, fame and a certain notoriety, spiritual crises and medical ones as well. There were periods when she must have feared her work was done, that she had used up her allotted time and talent without ever quite hitting her stride. But always there would have been the memory of the West, its unrealized promise, even in the dark hours of 1933 when she was deep into her own private depression. Even then she surely remembered that there was much more to America than skyscrapers and salons, summerhouses and mountain greenery. In coming to Taos in 1929 she had felt a clear confirmation of what she'd always at some level known, thus her instantaneous recognition of the country as hers. Then, in the blaze of August 1934, when she discovered Ghost Ranch, like some *nueva conquistadora*, she entered into her true and final domain.

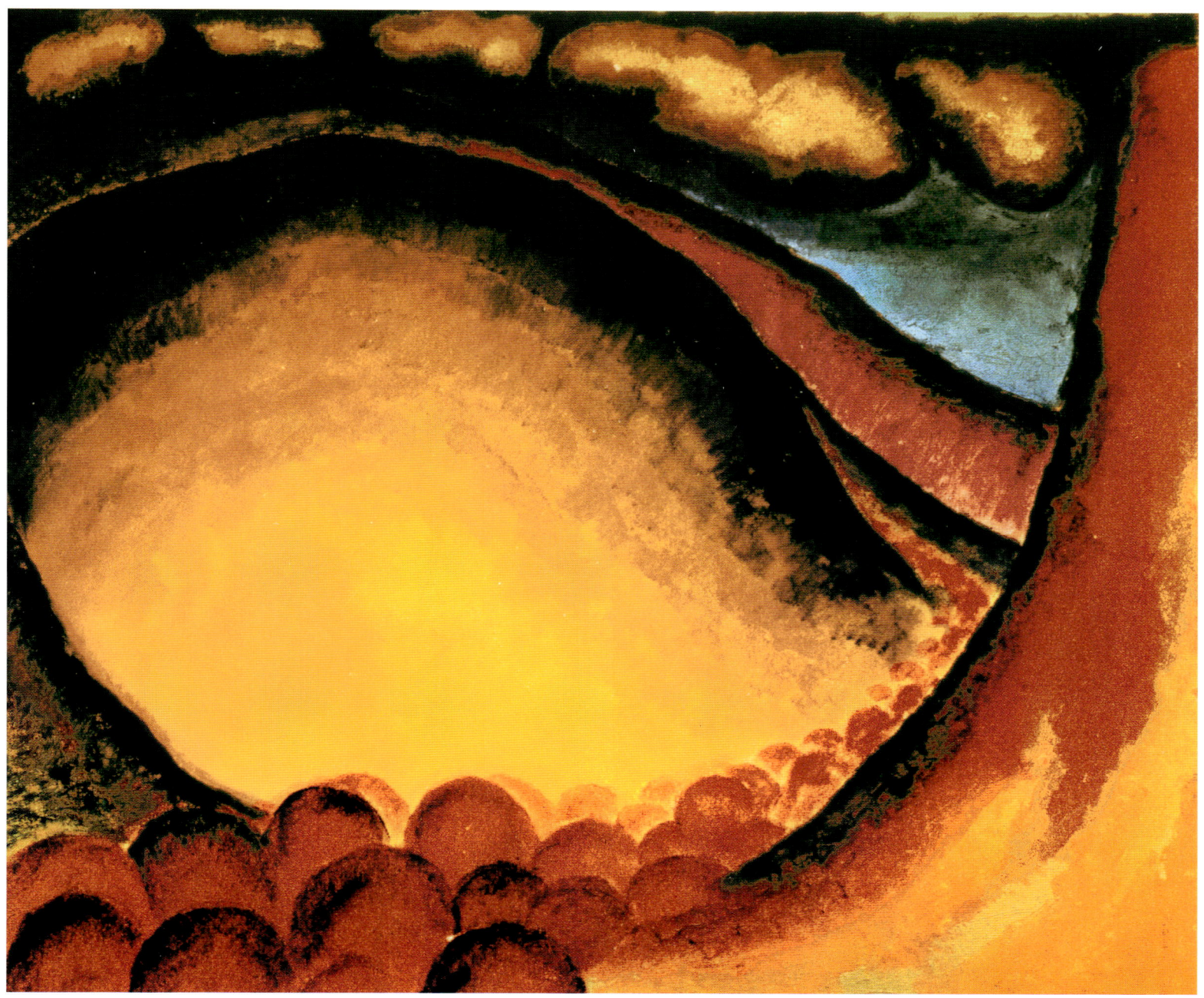

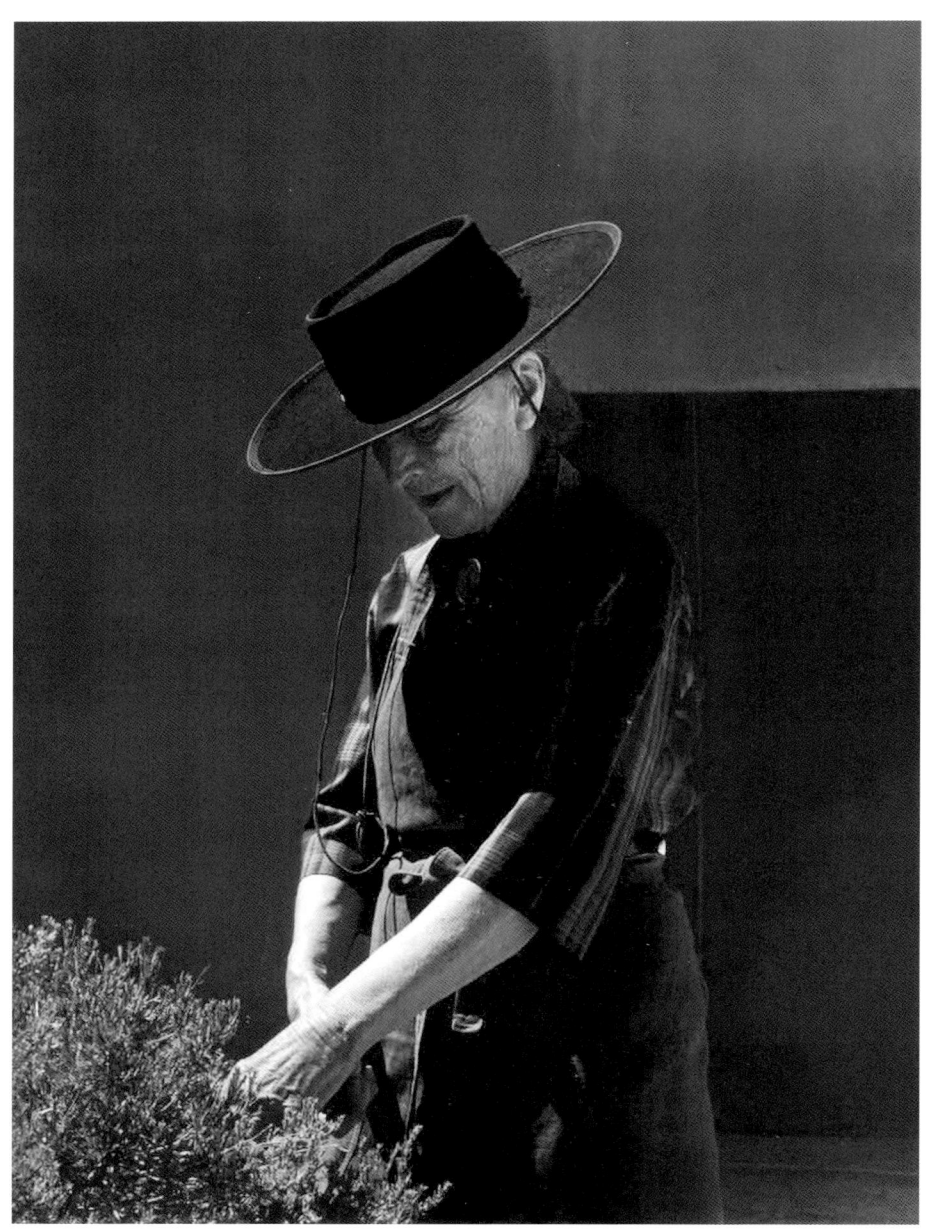

1887   November 15: Georgia Totto O'Keeffe born on a farm near Sun Prairie, Wisconsin.

1905–6   Attends School of The Art Institute of Chicago.

1907–8   Attends The Art Students League, New York.

1914–15   Attends Teachers College, Columbia University, New York.

1916   May: Alfred Stieglitz opens a group show at his gallery, known as 291, that includes
              some of O'Keeffe's work.

              Fall: Accepts teaching position at West Texas State Normal College, Canyon, Texas.

1917   April: Stieglitz opens *Georgia O'Keeffe*, the first one-person show of her work, at 291.

              August: Vacations in and around Ward, Colorado, and on return to Texas spends several
              days in Santa Fe, New Mexico.

1918   June: Moves to New York at Stieglitz's invitation, and for the next eleven years lives
              either in the city (winter and spring) or at Lake George, New York (summer and
              fall), with occasional excursions to, among other places, Maine, Washington, D.C.,
              and Wisconsin.

1923   January: Stieglitz opens *Alfred Stieglitz Presents One Hundred Pictures: Oils, Water-
              Colors, Pastels, Drawings, by Georgia O'Keeffe, American*, at The Anderson Galleries. He
              subsequently organizes exhibitions of her work annually until his death in 1946.

1924   December 11: Marries Alfred Stieglitz.

1929   April–August: Travels to Santa Fe; after arrival, moves to Taos as guest of Mabel Dodge
              Luhan, who provides O'Keeffe with a studio.

1930   Late April–August: Is in New Mexico; stays either with Luhan or at the H. and M. Ranch,
              as guest of Marie Tudor Garland.

OPPOSITE, FIG. 24
Todd Webb, *O'Keeffe in Patio,
Abiquiu House*, 1963

1932	June and August: Travels to Canada to paint.
1933	February: Is admitted to Doctor's Hospital, New York, suffering from psychoneurosis.
1934	January: Begins painting after a thirteen-month hiatus.
	June–October: Is in New Mexico.
	August: Makes first visit to Ghost Ranch, a dude ranch owned by Arthur Pack, located north of the village of Abiquiu.
1935	July–November: Is in New Mexico at Ghost Ranch.
1936	June–September: Is in New Mexico; spends her first summer living at Rancho de los Burros, the house at Ghost Ranch that she buys in 1940. She subsequently lives there almost every summer until 1949, when she moves to New Mexico permanently.
1937	July–October: Is in New Mexico.
1938	August–November: Is in New Mexico.
1939	Late January–April: Travels to Hawaii to paint, as a guest of Dole Pineapple Company.
1940	June–November: Is in New Mexico; buys Rancho de los Burros.
	October: Meets Maria Chabot, an aspiring writer, who lives summers with O'Keeffe until 1945, managing the house at Ghost Ranch and facilitating painting trips to the Black Place and the White Place.
1941	May–November: Is in New Mexico.
1942	June–November: Is in New Mexico.
1943	April–October: Is in New Mexico.
1944	April–October: Is in New Mexico.
1945	May–November: Is in New Mexico.
	December: After return to New York, purchases a ruined hacienda in Abiquiu.

1946	June: Is in New Mexico; Chabot begins renovating the Abiquiu hacienda, which she completes in 1949.
	July 13: Stieglitz dies.
	Late September–November: Is in New Mexico.
1947	January–early summer: Is in New York (where she primarily lives until 1949), working to settle the Stieglitz estate.
	August–December: Is in New Mexico.
1948	April–October: Is in New Mexico.
1949	June: Moves permanently to New Mexico, spending part of each year at either the Ghost Ranch or Abiquiu properties.
1971	Early in year: Loses central vision; retains only peripheral sight.
1973	Meets the artist Juan Hamilton, who teaches her to work with clay; he becomes her assistant, close friend, and later, her representative.
1984	Moves to a house known as Sol y Sombra in Santa Fe.
1986	March 6: Dies at St. Vincent's Hospital, Santa Fe.

CHECKLIST

1
Ranchos Church, Taos, 1929
Oil on canvas
24 x 36 in. (61 x 91.4 cm)
The Phillips Collection, Washington, D.C.
CR 662
See plate 18

2
Ranchos Church No. I, 1929
Oil on canvas
18 3/4 x 24 in. (47.6 x 61 cm)
Norton Museum of Art, West Palm Beach, Fla.
CR 664
See plate 19

3
Soft Grey Alcalde Hill, 1929/1930
Oil on canvas
10 1/8 x 24 1/8 in. (25.7 x 61.3 cm)
Hirshhorn Museum and Sculpture Garden,
Smithsonian Institution, Washington, D.C.
Gift of Joseph H. Hirshhorn, 1972
CR 691
See plate 24

4
Taos Pueblo, 1929/1934
Oil on canvas
24 x 40 in. (61 x 101.6 cm)
Eiteljorg Museum of American Indians
and Western Art, Indianapolis
CR 699
See plate 20

5
*Black Mesa Landscape, New Mexico / Out Back
of Marie's II*, 1930
Oil on canvas
24 1/4 x 36 1/4 in. (65.1 x 92.1 cm)
Georgia O'Keeffe Museum, Santa Fe, N. Mex.
Gift of The Burnett Foundation
CR 730
See plate 1

6
Dark Mesa with Pink Sky, 1930
Oil on canvas
16 1/4 x 30 3/8 in. (41.3 x 77.2 cm)
Amon Carter Museum, Fort Worth
CR 739
See plate 27

7
Hills Before Taos, 1930
Oil on canvas
16 x 30 in. (40.6 x 76.2 cm)
Montgomery Museum of Fine Arts, Ala.
The Blount Collection
CR 741
See plate 21

8
Near Abiquiu, N.M. 2, 1930
Oil on canvas
10 x 24 1/8 in. (25.4 x 61.3 cm)
The Metropolitan Museum of Art, New York.
Alfred Stieglitz Collection, 1963 (63.204)
CR 735
See plate 7

9
New Mexican Landscape, 1930
Oil on canvas
16 x 30 in. (40.6 x 76.2 cm)
Museum of Fine Arts, Springfield, Mass.
James Philip Gray Collection
CR 732
See plate 2

10
New Mexico Landscape and Sand Hills, 1930
Oil on canvas
16 x 30 in. (40.6 x 76.2 cm)
Private collection
CR 725
See plate 25

11
New Mexico Landscape, Mesa with Low Hills, 1930
Oil on canvas
10 x 15 in. (25.4 x 38.1 cm)
Private collection, Vt.
CR 736
See plate 9

12
Red Hills Beyond Abiquiu, 1930
Oil on canvas
30 x 36 in. (76.2 x 91.4 cm)
Eiteljorg Museum of American Indians
and Western Art, Indianapolis
CR 743
See plate 39

13
Rust Red Hills, 1930
Oil on canvas
16 x 30 in. (40.6 x 76.2 cm)
Brauer Museum of Art, Valparaiso University, Ind.
Sloan Fund Purchase, 62.02
CR 740
See plate 23

14
Taos Mountain, New Mexico, 1930
Oil on canvas
16 x 30 in. (40.6 x 76.2 cm)
Hood Museum of Art, Dartmouth College,
Hanover, N.H. Gift of M. Rosalie Leidinger
and Louise W. Schmidt
CR 742
See plate 22

15
Back of Marie's No. 4, 1931
Oil on canvas
16 x 30 in. (40.6 x 76.2 cm)
Georgia O'Keeffe Museum, Santa Fe, N. Mex.
Gift of The Burnett Foundation
CR 793
See plate 26

16
Near Abiquiu, New Mexico, 1931
Oil on canvas
16 x 36 in. (40.6 x 91.4 cm)
Private collection
CR 794
See plate 8

17
The Mountain, New Mexico, 1931
Oil on canvas
30 x 36 in. (76.2 x 91.4 cm)
Whitney Museum of American Art, New York.
Purchase 32.14
CR 790
See plate 38

18
Lavender Hill Forms, 1934
Oil on canvas
16 x 30 in. (40.6 x 76.2 cm)
Private collection
CR 836
See plate 10

19
Purple Hills Ghost Ranch—2 / Purple Hills No. II, 1934
Oil on canvas
16 1/4 x 30 1/4 in. (41.3 x 76.8 cm)
Georgia O'Keeffe Museum, Santa Fe, N. Mex.
Gift of The Burnett Foundation
CR 837
See plate 11

20
Small Purple Hills, 1934
Oil on board
16 x 19 3/4 in. (40.6 x 50.2 cm)
Private collection
CR 838
See plate 29

21
Chama River, Ghost Ranch, N. Mex., 1934/1935
Oil on canvas
30 x 16 in. (76.2 x 40.6 cm)
Private collection
CR 851
See plate 35

22
Hill, New Mexico, 1935
Oil on canvas
30 x 40 in. (76.2 x 101.6 cm)
Private collection
CR 872
See plate 3

23
Purple Hills, 1935
Oil on canvas
16 x 30 in. (40.6 x 76.2 cm)
San Diego Museum of Art. Gift of
Mr. and Mrs. Norton S. Walbridge
CR 870
See plate 28

24
Red Hills Series II, 1935/1938
Oil on canvas
16 x 30 in. (40.6 x 76.2 cm)
Museum of Texas Tech University, Lubbock
CR 875
See plate 47

25
Grey Hill Forms, 1936
Oil on canvas
20 x 30 in. (50.8 x 76.2 cm)
Museum of Fine Arts, Museum of New Mexico,
Santa Fe. Gift of the Estate of Georgia O'Keeffe,
1987 (87.449.1). By agreement between Museum
of New Mexico and The University of New Mexico,
in permanent possession of University Art
Museum, The University of New Mexico (P87.1)
CR 895
See plate 30

26
Pedernal, New Mexico, 1936
Oil on canvas
10 1/8 x 12 1/8 in. (25.7 x 30.8 cm)
Private collection
CR 901
See plate 41

27
Red Hills with Pedernal, White Clouds, 1936
Oil on canvas
20 x 30 in. (50.8 x 76.2 cm)
Private collection
CR 899
See plate 42

28
Cedar Tree with Lavender Hills, 1937
Oil on canvas
30 x 19 1/2 in. (76.2 x 49.5 cm)
Private collection
CR 935
See plate 12

29
Part of the Cliffs, 1937
Oil on canvas
20 x 32 in. (50.8 x 81.3 cm)
Private collection
CR 931
See plate 5

30
Red Hills and White Flower, 1937
Pastel on paper
19 3/8 x 25 5/8 in. (74.6 x 65.1 cm)
Georgia O'Keeffe Museum, Santa Fe, N. Mex.
Gift of The Burnett Foundation
CR 925
See plate 40

31
Red Hills, Blue Sky, 1937
Oil on canvas
9 x 14 in. (22.9 x 35.6 cm)
Herbert F. Johnson Museum of Art,
Cornell University, Ithaca, N.Y. Dr. and Mrs.
Milton Lurie Kramer (Class of 1936) Collection:
Bequest of Helen Kroll Kramer
CR 927
See plate 43

32
Red Hills No. I—New Mexico, 1937
Oil on canvas
16 x 36 in. (40.6 x 91.4 cm)
Bedford Family Collection
CR 928
See plate 44

33
My Red Hills, 1938
Oil on canvas
19 x 36 in. (48.3 x 91.4 cm)
Private collection
CR 954
See plate 13

34
The Cliff Chimneys, 1938
Oil on canvas
36 x 30 in. (91.4 x 76.2 cm)
Milwaukee Art Museum. Gift of Jane Bradley Pettit
Foundation and The Georgia O'Keeffe Foundation
CR 955
See plate 4

35
From The White Place, 1940
Oil on canvas
30 x 24 in. (76.2 x 61 cm)
The Phillips Collection, Washington, D.C.
CR 996
See plate 14

36
Patio No. II, 1940
Oil on canvas
24 x 19 in. (61 x 76.2 cm)
Jean and Alvin Snowiss Collection
CR 985
See plate 33

37
Stump in Red Hills, 1940
Oil on canvas
30 x 24 in. (76.2 x 61 cm)
Georgia O'Keeffe Museum, Santa Fe, N. Mex.
Gift of The Stéphane Janssen Trust
in memory of R. Michael Johns
CR 999
See plate 49

38
Untitled (Red and Yellow Cliffs), 1940
Oil on canvas
24 x 36 in. (61 x 91.4 cm)
Georgia O'Keeffe Museum, Santa Fe, N. Mex.
Gift of The Burnett Foundation
CR 998
See plate 6

39
Blue Sky, 1941
Oil on canvas
36 x 16 in. (91.4 x 40.6 cm)
Worcester Art Museum, Mass. Gift of
Mr. and Mrs. Robert W. Stoddard
CR 1028
See plate 36

40
Grey Hills, 1941
Oil on canvas
20 x 30 in. (50.8 x 76.2 cm)
Indianapolis Museum of Art. Gift of
Mr. and Mrs. James W. Fesler
CR 1024
See plate 16

41
Near Abiquiu, New Mexico, 1941
Oil on canvas
12 x 30 in. (30.5 x 76.2 cm)
Private collection
CR 1026
See plate 45

42
Red Hills and Bones, 1941
Oil on canvas
30 x 40 in. (76.2 x 101.6 cm)
Philadelphia Museum of Art.
Alfred Stieglitz Collection
CR 1025
See plate 48

43
White Place in Shadow, 1941
Oil on canvas
19 x 10 in. (48.3 x 25.4 cm)
Private collection
CR 1027
See plate 15

44
Cliffs Beyond Abiquiu—Dry Waterfall, 1943
Oil on canvas
30 x 16 in. (76.2 x 40.6 cm)
The Cleveland Museum of Art.
Bequest of Georgia O'Keeffe, 1987.141
CR 1061
See plate 32

45
The White Place—A Memory, 1943
Oil on canvas
30 x 20 in. (76.2 x 50.8 cm)
Private collection
CR 1062
See plate 37

46
Untitled (Dry Waterfall, Ghost Ranch), c. 1943
Graphite and charcoal on paper
23 7/8 x 17 7/8 in. (60.6 x 45.4 cm)
Georgia O'Keeffe Museum, Santa Fe, N. Mex.
Gift of The Burnett Foundation
CR 1071
See plate 34

47
Black Place III, 1944
Oil on canvas
36 x 40 in. (91.4 x 101.6 cm)
Georgia O'Keeffe Museum, Santa Fe, N. Mex.
Promised gift of The Burnett Foundation
CR 1082
See plate 17

48
Pedernal, 1945
Pastel on paper
21 1/2 x 43 1/4 in. (54.6 x 109.9 cm)
Georgia O'Keeffe Museum, Santa Fe, N. Mex.
Promised gift of The Burnett Foundation
CR 1117
See frontispiece

49
The Black Place III, 1945
Pastel on paper
27 3/4 x 43 3/4 in. (70.5 x 111.1 cm)
Private collection
CR 1112
See plate 31

50
Dry Waterfall, 1951
Oil on canvas
26 x 16 in. (66 x 40.6 cm)
Collection of Emily Fisher Landau
CR 1226
See plate 46

SUGGESTIONS FOR FURTHER READING

Atlanta Art Association. *Landscape into Art*. Exh. cat. Atlanta: Atlanta Art Association Galleries, 1962.

Casey, Edward S. *The Fate of Place: A Philosophical History*. Berkeley and Los Angeles: University of California Press, 1997.

Clark, Kenneth. *Landscape into Art*. New York: Harper & Row, 1976.

Collins, Jane Downer. "Georgia O'Keeffe and the New Mexico Landscape." Master's thesis, George Washington University, 1980.

Eldredge, Charles C. *Georgia O'Keeffe*. Library of American Art Series. New York: Harry N. Abrams; Washington, D.C.: The National Museum of American Art, Smithsonian Institution, 1991.

Lynes, Barbara Buhler. *O'Keeffe, Stieglitz, and the Critics, 1916–1929*. Ann Arbor: UMI Research Press, 1989. Reprint, Chicago: University of Chicago Press, 1991.

———. "The Language of Criticism: Its Effect on the Art of Georgia O'Keeffe in the 1920s." In *Georgia O'Keeffe: From the Faraway, Nearby*, ed. Ellen Bradbury and Christopher Merrill. Reading, Mass.: Addison-Wesley Press, 1992. Reprinted in *Women's Art Magazine*, no. 51 (Mar.–Apr. 1993): 4–9.

———. *Georgia O'Keeffe*. New York: Rizzoli International Publications, Inc., 1993.

———. *Georgia O'Keeffe: Catalogue Raisonné*. New Haven, Conn.: Yale University Press; Washington, D.C.: National Gallery of Art; Abiquiu, N. Mex.: The Georgia O'Keeffe Foundation, 1999.

Messinger, Lisa Mintz. *Georgia O'Keeffe*. New York: Thames and Hudson and The Metropolitan Museum of Art, 1988.

Mitchell, W. J. Thomas. *Landscape and Power*. 2nd ed. Chicago: University of Chicago Press, 2002.

O'Keeffe, Georgia. *Georgia O'Keeffe*. 1976. Reprint, New York: Penguin Books, 1985.

Peridot Gallery. *The American Landscape: A Living Tradition*. Exh. cat. New York: Peridot Gallery, 1968.

Peters, Sarah Whitaker. *Becoming O'Keeffe: The Early Years*. Rev. ed. New York: Abbeville Press, 2001.

Robinson, Roxana. *Georgia O'Keeffe: A Life*. New York: Harper & Row, 1989.

Shizuota Prefectual Museum. *Landscape Painting in the East and West*. Exh. cat. Shizuota, Japan: Shizuota Prefectual Museum, 1986.

Stebbins, Theodore E., Jr. "The Memory and the Present: Romantic American Painting in the Lane Collection." In *The Lane Collection: 20th-Century Paintings in the American Tradition,* by Theodore E. Stebbins, Jr., and Carol Troyen. Boston: Museum of Fine Arts, 1983.

Udall, Sharyn R. "Models of Consciousness: Myth and Memory in the Work of Georgia O'Keeffe, Eliot Porter, and Todd Webb." Chap. 6 in *Contested Terrain: Myth and Meanings in Southwest Art.* Albuquerque: University of New Mexico Press, 1996.

ACKNOWLEDGMENTS

The efforts of many individuals have made this exhibition and its catalogue possible, and I am deeply grateful for their help and collaboration. First and foremost, I want to thank the many collectors and institutions who have loaned to the exhibition and provided permission to reproduce their works in its catalogue: at the Amon Carter Museum, Fort Worth, Courtney DeAngelis Morfeld, Rick Stewart, Melissa G. Thompson; the Bedford Family Collection; at the Brauer Museum of Art, Valparaiso University, Ind., Gregg Hertzlieb, Gloria Ruff; at The Cleveland Museum of Art, Henry Adams, Henry Hawley, Tom Hinson, Katharine Lee Reid, Gretchen Shie, Mary Suzor, Monica Wolf; at the Eiteljorg Museum of American Indians and Western Art, Indianapolis, Becky Hutchins, James Nottage, Sara Summers, John Vanausdall; at The Georgia O'Keeffe Foundation, Abiquiu, N. Mex., Agapita Judy Lopez; at the Herbert F. Johnson Museum of Art, Cornell University, Ithaca, N.Y., Warren Bunn, Frank Robinson, Whitney Tassie; at the Hirshhorn Museum and Sculpture Garden, Smithsonian Institution, Washington, D.C., Amy Densford, Brian G. Kavanagh, Ned Rifkin, Phyllis Rosenzweig; at the Hood Museum of Art, Dartmouth College, Hanover, N.H., Juliette Bianco, Derrick R. Cartwright, Cynthia Gilliland, Kellen Haak, Barbara MacAdam, Kathleen P. O'Malley; at the Indianapolis Museum of Art, Anthony Hirschel, Rebekah Marshall, Ruth V. Roberts; at the Los Angeles County Museum of Art, Michelle Ahern, Shaula Coyl, Andrea Rich; the Collection of Emily Fisher Landau; at The Metropolitan Museum of Art, New York, Ida Balboul, Minora Collins, Deanna Cross, Philippe de Montebello, Peter M. Kenny, Lisa Messinger; at the Milwaukee Art Museum, Leigh Albritton, Russell Bowman, Brian Ferriso, Poorima Moorthy; at the Montgomery Museum of Fine Arts, Ala., Margaret Lynne Ausfeld, Pam Bransford, Alice Carter, Mark Johnson; at the Museum of Fine Arts, Museum of New Mexico, Santa Fe, Marsha C. Bol, Joan Tafoya; at the Museum of Fine Arts, Springfield, Mass., Barbara Plante, Heather R. Haskell, Wendy Stayman; at the Museum of Texas Tech University, Lubbock, Gary Edson, Nicky Ladkin, Bill Mueller; at the Norton Museum of Art, West Palm Beach, Fla., Sandra Barghini, Lisa Heard, Christina Orr-Cahall, Pamela Parry, Roger Ward; at the Philadelphia Museum of Art, Stacey Bomento, Amy P. Dowe, Anne d'Harnoncourt, Irene Torrance; at

The Phillips Collection, Jay Gates, Joseph Holbach, Christopher Ketcham, Elizabeth Hutton Turner; at the San Diego Museum of Art, Don Bacigalupi, Tammie Bennett, Louis Goldich, David L. Kencik; the Jean and Alvin Snowiss Collection; at the University Art Museum, The University of New Mexico, Albuquerque, Linda W. Bahm, Bonnie Verardo; at the Whitney Museum of American Art, New York, Maxwell Anderson, Jennifer Belt, Barbara Haskell, Joelle LaFerrara, Barbi Spieler; and at the Worcester Art Museum, Mass., Selina Bartlett, David Brigham, Nancy L. Swallow, James A. Welu.

At the Georgia O'Keeffe Museum, Santa Fe, I wish to thank the Board of Directors, The Burnett Foundation, and the National Council of the Georgia O'Keeffe Museum for their generous support of this exhibition. In addition, I thank George G. King, director, Jenifer Jovais, exhibitions coordinator, Dale Kronkright, conservator, Judy Smith, registrar, and Michael Shiller, preparator.

I am also grateful to Corbis; the Deborah Force Gallery; Deborah Ronnen Fine Art; the Evans Gallery; Getty Images; Irene Drori, Inc.; the John Berggruen Gallery; Spanierman Gallery LLC; Time Life Pictures, Time Inc.; and Kathy Chilton, who designed the map in this book. Also my thanks to photographers Mark Kane, Herbert Lotz, and Malcolm Varon; and to editor Susan Heard.

At Princeton University Press, I wish to thank Nancy Grubb and her colleagues, Cynthia Grow, Sarah Henry, Devra K. Nelson, Ken Wong, and Kate Zanzucchi. I also wish to acknowledge the very capable freelancers engaged by Princeton: Alison Rooney, copyeditor; Joel Avirom, designer; June Cuffner, proofreader; and Cathy Dorsey, indexer.

Barbara Buhler Lynes

INDEX

Page numbers in *italics* refer to illustrations

Abiquiu, N. Mex., 79
    O'Keeffe's home in, 87, 126, 127
    paintings of, *94, 95*
abstraction, 11–13
    ambiguities between two- and three-
        dimensional elements and, 21, 36–38
    cropping and, 21, 28, 45, 51
    dynamic linear rhythms and, 21, 28
    faithfulness to primary contours and, 13, 16, 34,
        45, 55
    interpreted as manifestation of O'Keeffe's
        sexual nature, 11, 56
    lighting effects and, 38
    magnification and, 29, 40
    photographic devices and, 51–56
    reduction and simplification of forms and, 17,
        21, 28–29
    size and scale manipulations and, 16, 51, 55
    spatial compression and, 16, 17, 21, 29, 36–38,
        40, 42, 45, 51, 114
    synthesis of points of view and, 40, 42–45
    tonal manipulation and, 21, 29, 31, 34, 36, 40,
        42, 46, 51, 52, 55
Adams, Ansel, *108,* 113–14
Alcalde, N. Mex., 14

paintings of, 14–16, *15, 67–69*
photograph of, *14*
An American Place (New York), 121
Anderson, Walter Inglis, 118
Asian art, 114
Aswell, Mary Lou, 109, 111

Back of Marie's No. 4, 69
Bement, Alon, 114
Bierstadt, Albert, 121
Black Mesa Landscape, New Mexico / Out Back of
    Marie's II, 14–16, *15,* 31
    photograph of site of, *14*
Black Place, 84–87, 126
    paintings of, 45–46, *48, 49, 74–75*
    photograph of, *48*
Black Place III (1944), 46, *49*
Black Place III, The (1945), *75*
Blue and Green Music, 44, *45*
Blue Sky, 92
Bodmer, Karl, 121
Brennan, Jim, 111
Burke, Kenneth, 121

Camera Work, 52
Cather, Willa, 78, 115
Cedar Tree with Lavender Hills, 34–38, *39*

photograph of site of, *38*

Cézanne, Paul, 118

Chabot, Maria, 87, 126

Chama River, 78, 79, 80, 118

    painting of, *91*

    photograph of, *50*

Chama River, Ghost Ranch, *91*

Chama Running Red (Sloan), 118

Chinle Formation, *81, 82, 83*

Chrysler Building Seen from the Shelton Hotel, The, *54, 55*

Cliff Chimneys, The, 20–21, 25

    photograph of site of, *24*

Cliffs Beyond Abiquiu—Dry Waterfall, *83*

color:

    in landscape surrounding Ghost Ranch, 31–32, 80

    tonal manipulation and, 21, 29, 31, 34, 36, 40, 42, 46, 51, 52, 55

contours, faithfulness to, 13, 16, 34, 45, 55

Cowley, Malcolm, 121

cropping, 21, 28, 45, 51

Dakota Formation, 81, *81*

Dark Mesa with Pink Sky, *71*

    photograph of site of, *32*

Democratic Vistas (Whitman), 120

Demuth, Charles, 121

Dove, Arthur, III, 120–21

Dow, Arthur, 114

Dry Waterfall, *103*

Duchamp, Marcel, 121

Emerson, Ralph Waldo, 120

Entrada Formation, *81, 82, 83*

Evening Walk, Ghost Ranch (Loengard), *76*

flower paintings, large-scale, 11, 29, 55

From the White Place, 42–45, *43*

    photograph of site of, *42*

Garland, Marie Tudor, 14, 125

Georgia O'Keeffe (Adams), *108*

Ghost Ranch, 12, 20, 80–84, 118, 122, 126, 127

    colors in landscape surrounding, 31–32, 80

    geologic layers in cliffs at, 80–84, *81, 82*

    O'Keeffe's home at, 84, 87, 126

    paintings and drawings of, *2*, 20–21, *23*, 25–27, 31–40, *35, 37, 39, 41, 72, 73, 83, 85, 86, 97–107*

    photographs of, *22, 24, 26, 36, 38, 40, 76*

Grey Hill Forms, *74*

Grey Hills, 45–46, *48*

    photograph of site of, *48*

Hall, Edward, 109

Hamilton, Juan, 127

H. and M. Ranch (Alcalde, N. Mex.), 14, 17, 125

Hartley, Marsden, 121

Hawthorne, Nathaniel, 120

Hemingway, Ernest, 116, 121

Hill, New Mexico, 20–21, *23*

    photograph of site of, *22*

Hills Before Taos, *64*

Homer, Winslow, 118

Hopper, Edward, 121

In the American Grain (Williams), 121

Jackson, John Brinkerhoff, 109
James, Bill, 109–11
James, Julie, 109–11

Lake George, 11, 12, 52, 122, 125
Lavender Hill Forms, 32, 34, *35*
    photograph of site of, *36*
Leigh, William Robinson, 121
lighting effects, 38
Loengard, John, *76*
Luhan, Mabel Dodge, 78, 125

MacLeish, Archibald, 119
magnification, 29, 40
Marin, John, 120–21
Masters, John, 109
McBride, Henry, 31
Monet, Claude, 118
Moonrise over Hernandez (Adams), 113–14
Moran, Thomas, 121
Morrison Formation, 81, *81*
Mountain, New Mexico, The, *94*
My Red Hills, 38–40, *41*
    photograph of site of, *40*

Near Abiquiu, New Mexico (1931), 28–29, *30*
    photograph of site of, *28*
Near Abiquiu, New Mexico (1941), *102*
Near Abiquiu, N.M. 2, 28, 29, 31

Newmann, Eugene, 113–19, 121
New Mexican Landscape, 17, *19*
    photograph of site of, *18*
New Mexico Landscape, Mesa with Low Hills, 31, *33*
    photograph of site of, *32*
New Mexico Landscape and Sand Hills, *68*
New York, 56, 79, 122, 125
    O'Keeffe's involvement with photography in, 51–55
    photographs of, *54*, *55*
    Stieglitz circle in, 120–21
No. 9 Special, 45
No. 21—Special, 122, *123*

O'Keeffe, Claudia, 78
O'Keeffe—Chama River—New Mexico (Webb), *50*
"O'Keeffe country," 12, 77–87, 109–22
    colors of, 31–32, 80
    geology of, 80–84, *81*, *82*
    nature of O'Keeffe's relationship to, 112–22
    O'Keeffe's relocation to, 78–80, 84–87, 125, 126
    O'Keeffe's social isolation in, 109–12, 113, 117
    topography of, 77–78
    visible tributes to O'Keeffe in, 111–12
    see also specific sites
O'Keeffe in Patio, Abiquiu House (Webb), *124*
O'Keeffe Walking in The White Place, Abiquiu, NM (Webb), *10*
O'Keeffe with her new Leica (Webb), *53*

Pack, Arthur, 84, 126
Part of the Cliffs, 20–21, 26

photograph of site of, *26*
Patio No. II, *85*
Pedernal, 77–78, 79–80, 84, 116, 117
    paintings of, *2*, *79*, *98*, *99*
Pedernal, *2*
Pedernal, New Mexico, *98*
Peters, Sarah Whitaker, 55
Phillips, Duncan, 111
Phillips, Gifford, 109, 111
Phillips, Joanne, 109, 111, 112
photography:
    abstraction in O'Keeffe's work related to
        devices of, 51–55
    O'Keeffe's familiarity with technical aspects of,
        52–53
Picasso, Pablo, 51
Plaza Colorado, 42
points of view, 51
    synthesis of, 40, 42–45
Pollitzer, Anita, 51
Porter, Aline, 109
Porter, Eliot, 109, 111
Pound, Ezra, 121
Purple Hills, *72*
Purple Hills Ghost Ranch—2 / Purple Hills No. II,
    32–34, *37*
    photograph of site of, *36*

Rancho de los Burros, 84, 87, 126
    painting of, *85*
Ranchos Church, Taos, *61*
Ranchos Church No. I, *62*
Red Hills, Blue Sky, *100*

Red Hills and Bones, *106*
Red Hills and White Flower, *97*
Red Hills Beyond Abiquiu, *95*
Red Hills No. I—New Mexico, *101*
Red Hills Series II, *105*
Red Hills with Pedernal, White Clouds, *99*
Rosenfeld, Paul, 52
Rust Red Hills, *66*

Saam, Sibyl, 111
Santa Fe, N. Mex.:
    O'Keeffe's first trip to, 78, 125
    O'Keeffe's home in, 110, 127
    visible tributes to O'Keeffe in, 111–12
Scott, Sam, 113–19
series, working in, 45, 51
Sims, Agi, 109, 111
size and scale manipulations and, 16, 51, 55
Sloan, John, 118
Small Purple Hills, *73*
Soft Grey Alcalde Hill, *67*
Sol y Sombra (Santa Fe, N. Mex.), 110, 127
Stearns, Harold, 121
Stein, Gertrude, 121
Stieglitz, Alfred, 51–55, 87, 112, 120–21, 125,
    126
Strand, Paul, 51–52, 120–21
Stump in Red Hills, *107*, *117*

Taos, 78–79, 114, 122, 125
Taos, N. Mex.:
    paintings of, 61–66
Taos Mountain, New Mexico, *65*

Taos Pueblo, 63
Thomson, Virgil, 121
Thoreau, Henry David, 120
Tierra Azul, 28
    paintings of, *17, 19, 28–31, 29, 30, 33, 71*
    photographs of, *18, 28, 32*
Todilto Formation, *81, 82,* 83
Toomer, Jean, 112
291 (New York), 51, 125

Ufer, Walter, 121
Untitled (Chrysler Building), 55
Untitled (Dry Waterfall, Ghost Ranch), 86
Untitled (Red and Yellow Cliffs), 20–21, 27
    photograph of site of, *26*

V-shapes, 45, 46

Webb, Todd, *10, 50,* 51, *53, 124*
Welty, Eudora, 109
White Place, 42–45, 87, 116, 126
    paintings of, 42–45, *43, 47, 92, 93*
    photographs of, *10, 42, 46*
White Place—A Memory, The, 93
White Place in Shadow, 45, *47*
    photograph of site of, *46*
Whitman, Walt, 120
Williams, William Carlos, 120, 121
Wisconsin, O'Keeffe's early years in, 119, 125

The photographers and the sources of visual material other than those indicated in the captions are as follows:

© 1997 Amon Carter Museum, Fort Worth. Photo: Steve Watson (plate 27)

© Ansel Adams Publishing Rights Trust/Corbis (fig. 22)

Ben Blackwell (plate 15)

© The Cleveland Museum of Art (plate 32)

Sheldan C. Collins (plate 38)

© Eiteljorg Museum of American Indians and Western Art, Indianapolis (plate 20)

© The Georgia O'Keeffe Foundation, Abiquiu, N. Mex. Photo: Malcolm Varon (plates 1, 6, 11, 29, 49; fig. 18)

© Georgia O'Keeffe Museum, Santa Fe, N. Mex. Photo: Malcolm Varon (plate 26)

© Juan Hamilton. Photo: Malcolm Varon (frontispiece, plates 17, 34, 40)

Mark Kane (figs. 2, 3, 7, 8, 12, 14)

Herbert Lotz (figs. 5, 6, 11, 15)

© 1984 The Metropolitan Museum of Art. Photo: Malcolm Varon (plate 7)

Quesada/Burke, NY (plate 41)

Larry Sanders (plate 4)

Steven Sloman (plates 19, 33)

David Stansbury (plate 2)

© Time Life Pictures/Getty Images. Photo: John Loengard (fig. 19)

© Todd Webb, Courtesy Evans Gallery and Todd Webb Trust, Portland, Maine (figs. 1, 16, 17, 24)

© Worcester Art Museum, Mass. (plate 36)

Malcolm Varon (plates 3, 8, 12, 18, 30, 35, 37, 46; figs. 4, 9, 10)

Designed by Joel Avirom

Design assistants: Jason Snyder and Meghan Day Healey

Composed by Tina Thompson

Separations, printing, and binding by Conti Tipocolor, Florence

Printed on 150gsm Gardamatt

ABOUT THE TYPE

The text was set in Scala,
designed in 1990 by Martin Majoor (born 1960)

The display typeface is Copperplate Gothic,
designed in 1901 by Frederic William Goudy (1865–1947)